Molder of Dreams

FOCUS ON THE FAMILY

Molder of Dreams

Guy Rice Doud

Tyndale House Publishers, Wheaton, Illinois

MOLDER OF DREAMS
Copyright © 1990 by Guy Doud

Library of Congress Cataloging-in-Publication Data

Doug, Guy Rice, 1953–
    Molder of dreams / Guy Rice Doud.
        p.   cm.
    ISBN 1-56179-649-2 : $11.99
    1. Doud, Guy Rice, 1953– —Childhood and youth. 2. Staples (Minn.)—Biography.
3. Christian biography—Minnesota—Staples. 4. Family—United States. I. Title.
F614.S82D68   1990
977.6'88—dc20   90-43631
[B]   CIP

A Focus on the Family Book Published by
Tyndale House Publishers, Wheaton, Illinois 60189

Editor: Janet Kobobel
Cover illustration: Wayne Wolfe
Book designer: Sherry Nicolai Russell
Printed in the United States of America

98 99 00 01/10 9 8 7

Dedication

To Guy and Mayme Rice, Grandma and Grandpa;
Jesse and Jeannette Doud, Mom and Dad;
And all the other molders of my dreams.

Contents

Foreword

Guy Doud is the best argument I know for Christians to teach in the public school system. He demonstrates that you do not have to read the Bible and pray before class to introduce children to God's love. This man prays *for* his students before he gets to school, and he lives out the biblical message before his students without ever having to quote a chapter or verse. He makes it clear that loving and caring in the name of Christ can be done even when the name of Christ is not mentioned. He shows us how to make a classroom into an evangelistic field even when there is not room for sermons.

I have been troubled by the way in which many contemporary evangelicals have put down teaching in the public school system. They have considered public schools to be secular-humanistic institutions that prohibit the communication of the Christian faith. Guy Doud challenges that judgment and demonstrates that, in reality, public schools are more neutral than that. Public schools do not allow proselytizing at the taxpayers' expense, but there is nothing to keep teachers from *being* Christian and maintaining a Christian life-style. There is nothing to keep teachers from evangelizing outside of the school and sharing their faith with students who are impressed with their love and concern.

I must admit that I am a bit irritated with those who suggest that, if evangelism cannot be carried on overtly and directly in the classroom, then there is no hope for ever reaching children and teenagers with the gospel. It is just not so. Teachers can communicate Christ to their students, but they can only do it after school and away from school, and then only after they have earned the right to be heard while they were in school.

Marshall McLuhan once said "the medium is the message." Quite simply, that means that what is really understood is not so much determined by the content of what is said as it is by the *means* or the *method* by which it is communicated. The love of Christ can come over, under and around the reciting of a secular poem or the presentation of a math problem. The caring of the caring Jesus can be the medium through which instruction is given in history or in art. Public school officials say that the content of what is taught must be religiously neutral, but they do not, indeed cannot, say that there can be no spirituality in the manner of teaching or in the demeanor of the teacher. When you finish reading this book, you will see how the latter can be achieved.

Recently, the Supreme Court of the United States guaranteed still another right of those in the public school system. It is now declared permissible to have religious meetings on the school campus as an after-school extra-curricular activity. That means that Christian teachers can be advisers for Bible studies, clubs that promote evangelism and Christian social action organizations. The school authorities cannot keep Christian activities out of the school. It is just that such activities cannot occur during class time. There is a great opportunity to infuse the public school system with a Christian presence, and this presents a brilliant challenge for Christians who want to make a difference for His kingdom.

Guy Doud is more than a symbol; he is a leader. He is a man committed to a movement that will extend an awareness of the Lordship of Christ in the schools throughout America. Men and women who want to be part of that movement should contact him and explore how they, too, can model Christ in the secular world of public education and make of school teaching a missionary venture. He is doing his best to inspire and challenge young people to consider the vocation which he has found to be a "high calling of God in Christ Jesus" (Phil. 3:14, KJV). He wants for such visionaries to be able to get together, reinforce each others' values and beliefs, and explore ways to carry out this mission. To such ends this book is a good beginning.

Tony Campolo
Sociologist, Author

Acknowledgments

I would like to thank the following. They, too, are molders of dreams:

Janet Kobobel and the entire staff at Focus on the Family. The family at Christ Community Church in Nisswa, especially my elder board, which stood with me in prayer.

Hope Lindman and Ray Frisch, who listened to me read.

Tony Campolo, Dr. Leo Buscaglia, Clark Mollenhoff, Tom Martin.

Seth, Luke, Jessica and Zachary, my children *and* my nephews and niece, who missed Dad when I had to be writing.

And, of course, Tammy, who hasn't molded my dreams so much as fulfilled them.

Introduction

I n the beginning God..."
That's a great way to begin a book.
It's a great way to begin a world.
Then came Adam. Then came Eve. Then came children.

Children grew up and gave birth to other children. If you read the King James Version, the word is "begat."

I love the words of King James. "Gave birth to" just doesn't seem as descriptive as "begat."

Abraham begat Isaac; and Isaac begat Jacob; and Jacob begat Judah...There's been a lot of "begetting" to get to where we are today.

Some who were begat we've forgotten. That doesn't mean they weren't important. Some who were begat we know only a little about.

My wife and I wanted biblical names for our children, so I looked through some of the begats in the Bible. "Shealtiel begat Zerubbabel." We didn't consider Zerubbabel. I'm not sure Zerubbabel liked his name either, because some people called him Sheshbazzar. We didn't consider Sheshbazzar either.

But Zerubbabel was a godly man. On the ruins of the temple that had been destroyed by Nebuchadnezzar (another interesting name), Zerubbabel erected an altar and laid the foundation for a new temple.

Zerubbabel was a foundation builder.

He was also a direct ancestor of the greatest foundation builder of all time.

After Zerubbabel died there was quite a bit more begetting until Judah begat Joseph. Joseph made a living as a carpenter and became the husband of Mary, of whom was born Jesus, who is called Christ.

Christ was born in a village that was "small among the clans of Judah" (Micah 5:2). He grew up in another village that no one thought would ever be important, either.

Jesus lived only about thirty-three years, but I think you know what He accomplished.

Many years have passed since Jesus walked the earth, and people have kept begetting. Somewhere in the process your grandparents were begotten, and your parents were begotten, and you were begotten.

You're a foundation builder, too.

You may think you live in a rather unimportant place or have an insignificant job, but what could be more important than helping to shape and mold others' lives? And that's exactly what you do.

God bless you, you molder of dreams!

Small Towns
and Grandparents

Someone once said you can take the boy out of the small town, but you can't take the small town out of the boy—or something like that. The small town in my life is Staples, Minnesota.

Staples never gets the recognition it deserves. Its neighbor, Lake Wobegon, over in Mist County, seems to have grabbed the national spotlight. But the women in Staples are just as strong, and the men are every bit as good looking as our famous neighbors.

I grew up in Staples. (And I know I'm above average!) There I played king of the mountain, made igloos and snowmen, faithfully delivered the Minneapolis *Star Tribune* for most of the south side, rode in the back of Charlie Page's pickup on Boy Scout paper drives, sang in the church choir, attended Lincoln Elementary and graduated from Staples High School.

Somewhere at the bottom of Dower Lake, just west of Staples, is my high school class ring. (Mine is the one with the red stone and diagonal inlaid mother-of-pearl stripes across the front. It also bears my initials "GRD" on the inside.) If you find it, I'm still offering a reward. I special-ordered the mother-of-pearl stripes so when you looked at my ring you would see red and white—the school colors.

As far as I know, my ring has been at the bottom of Dower Lake ever since July 1971. I graduated from Staples High School in May 1971, so I didn't get to wear the ring very long. How my ring was lost in Dower Lake is best left undisclosed, unless, of course, you want the version I gave my parents, who, when they paid for the ring, had made some comment about robbing a bank.

There is still lots of small town in me—always will be. Much of what I am was shaped by my family, my teachers, my peers and my experiences growing up in Staples.

I don't know how growing up in Staples compares with growing up where you did, but I suspect there are many similarities. Even if you grew up in a large city, certain people were there when you were a kid—people who made a lasting impression. They are the people who taught you something about life you've never forgotten. If you sat down right now to make a list, these are the people you would put on it.

The funny thing is these people might not even know they're on the list. For instance, Roy Hill and Budd Lindaman are on my list, and I'm sure they don't know it.

Like me, you learned good things from some people, and you learned bad things from others. I learned good things from Roy Hill and Budd Lindaman.

They were the two janitors at Lincoln Elementary School. They were nice guys and treated kids with respect. They had time to stop, lean on their brooms and tell you a joke.

I remember Mr. Hill looking at me and asking, "Did you hear the one about. . ."

Mr. Lindaman always seemed to appear immediately after some

kid, sick with the flu or with an upset stomach from a rigorous recess, had deposited his lunch on the classroom floor. Mr. Lindaman would spread the sawdustlike, smelly stuff over the accident spot. He cleaned it up with a smile and never seemed to mind.

I think every kid at Lincoln loved both Mr. Hill and Mr. Lindaman. I learned from them that you could be happy at your work, and if you were nice to people and treated others with respect, about ninety-five percent of the time people treated you with respect as well.

Fern Kelsey is on the list, too. Fern, or "Ferny" as I came to call her, was my grandparents' friend and neighbor. She also attended the same church we did. She was like another grandmother to me.

In my early days at Lincoln Elementary, Ferny was one of the school cooks, and every day I would get a hug and a kiss from her as I went through the lunch line. I looked forward to lunch.

Ferny's husband had died, and she often joined our family for Thanksgiving, Christmas and Easter dinners. She was also invited to dinner on other special occasions, and whenever she would come, she would bring her homemade biscuits, which she called "scones."

My, how I loved Ferny's scones! I would eat a dozen of them.

If I can digress just a bit here, I might mention that to this day I remember Fern Kelsey's scones every major holiday. A few years ago on Thanksgiving, I asked my wife, Tammy, to try her hand at making scones just like Ferny's. My sisters were both joining us for Thanksgiving dinner, and I knew they loved Ferny's scones as much as I did.

Well, the drippings from the turkey caused problems in the oven. The aluminum roaster the turkey was in began to leak, and the smoke billowed from the oven. In the process of trying to transplant the turkey to a different roaster, the scones were forgotten and not remembered until the oven started on fire. We're still not sure whether the fire was caused by the turkey drippings or the scones, which left unattended, suddenly burst into flames.

Regardless, this all happened about the time my sister Janice and her husband, Jerry, arrived for dinner. They had driven up from Minneapolis. We were excited to have them join us, as they had never been to our home for dinner before—let alone Thanksgiving dinner.

My eldest son, Seth, who was five at the time, greeted them at the door and told them dinner was almost ready. They entered a house rapidly filling with smoke.

Janice asked, "What's all the smoke?"

Seth answered, "Oh, Mom's just cooking."

Tammy was frantically trying to extinguish the flames and wasn't even aware that Jan and Jerry had arrived. She removed the scones and drowned the fire with a box of baking soda. The fire was extinguished, but of course, the scones were ruined.

I looked at them sitting on the counter. They were as black as Seth's new dress shoes. Tammy regretfully—almost ceremoniously—carried them to the garbage can in the garage, greeting my sister and her husband as she passed by.

I thought I had seen the last of those scones. But Janice, unbeknown to Tammy or me, stole the burnt scones out of our trash can and took them home with her.

Just before Christmas, Tammy received a package in the mail. The package, beautifully wrapped in Christmas paper, contained a burnt scone wreath. My sister had taken the burnt buns, glued them to a circular mold, shellacked them, and added holly and ivy.

That was Tammy's first attempt at making scones. It was also her last. I have the entire event on videotape, if you would care to see it.

Ferny knew how much I loved scones, but I bet she would have never guessed that someday I would have a wreath made out of them.

A few years ago, I sang at Ferny's funeral on the Fourth of July, and I couldn't help but remember her scones, which really were symbols of her love, her way of saying thanks for including her as part of our family—which she indeed had become.

Ferny taught me that even if your spouse dies, you're still part of a bigger family. And in the same way you need other people to show you love and take you in, those same people may be waiting for you to show them love and include you in their lives.

Sometimes I've wondered how I would have survived those days at Lincoln without the jokes of Mr. Hill, the smiles and quiet voice of Mr. Lindaman, and the hugs and kisses from Ferny. I'm glad I'll never have to know.

Staples was the kind of place a kid like me could pick up the phone and say, "I want to talk to my grandma." And the town operator, Maude Dahl, knew who I was and who my grandma was, and would say, "Just a minute, Guy, and I'll ring your grandma for you."

Maude Dahl is on my list, too. And of course, so are my grandparents.

What I'm trying to say here is that no matter where you grew up, the people on your list had a tremendous influence on you—they helped shape and mold your life and your dreams. And when you grow up, you're going to be on someone's list as well.

The rest of this book is about that very subject—how your life affects the lives of others, and how others have affected you. This is especially significant if you have felt the call of Christ in your life and have sought to be His light in the world.

You can't help but be a witness; your very life is a letter that others read, and you are writing messages on the tablets of their hearts. The apostle Paul writes to the church in Corinth: "You yourselves are our letter, written on our hearts, known and read by everybody. You show that you are a letter from Christ, the result of our ministry, written not with ink but with the Spirit of the living God, not on tablets of stone but on tablets of human hearts" (2 Cor. 3:2-3).

Have you ever stopped to wonder whose letters you've read to lead you to believe what you do today? Have you stopped to consider what kind of letter you are writing on others' hearts?

Forgive me for being so direct, but those are important questions, and I feel better being up-front in asking them. I guess that's another quality I learned in Staples.

Yes, I learned lots of lessons from the letters I read while growing up. I thank God for all the positive witnesses that have helped shape my life, but I mentioned earlier that we also learn some bad things from others.

I think I learned my share—and then some—of bad things. I read many bad letters that tried to convince me my life didn't really matter, that I wasn't quite acceptable.

I have always instinctively believed that people actually begin to be influenced by the letters of others' lives from the time they are in the womb. Recently I read of research that confirms this. We now know, of course, that the mother's diet and life-style during pregnancy can do much to influence the health of the child after birth.

With birth comes an onslaught of learning, and the community, the family, and all those significant others teach a child from the very beginning whether he or she is welcome, loved and accepted.

An important part of the early learning experience is shaped by the environment and community in which the child is raised. Staples is in central Minnesota about 130 miles north of Minneapolis-St. Paul. The area is mostly identified with lakes, fishing and agriculture, but Staples was put on the map because of the railroad, and the railroad accounts for my being raised there.

Ours was a railroad family. My grandfather, Guy Rice, was born just outside Staples in 1886. Grandpa Guy grew up and went to work for the Northern Pacific Railroad in 1905. He met and courted Mayme Tooley, and they were married in 1913. They established their home in Staples, which was and still is one of the major division points for the railroad.

They raised three daughters: Fern, Jeannette and Renee. Jeannette was my mom, who was born in 1918 and married Jesse Doud in 1947. I, their first child, was born in October 1953. Jesse, my father, worked for the railroad at that time, too, so that's why I say the railroad is responsible for my being raised in Staples.

You may have noticed the similarity between my grandfather's name and mine. It's because—as my mother told it—Grandpa showed up at the hospital, and although he was happy that my parents had chosen Guy for my first name, he thought Rice, his last name, would make a better middle name than Ronald, which my folks had chosen. My parents had chosen Ronald because my father had a son named Ronald from a previous marriage. Ronald had died of spinal meningitis at age seven.

But my grandfather was quite insistent that if I was going to be named after him, my folks should go all the way and add the Rice as well. It was important to him, Mom said, because he was the only male child in his family, and he and Mayme had no sons. Making Rice my middle name would do a little something to perpetuate his family name, he felt.

In my baby book, you can see where my mother crossed out "Ronald" and wrote in "Rice." I grew up believing my name was Guy Rice Doud.

That is my name now and has been ever since 1988. In the process of applying for my first passport, I received the necessary copy of my birth certificate from the courthouse and was surprised to see that, according to Wadena County and the State of Minnesota, I was Guy Ronald Doud.

Mom may have changed my name in her baby book, but according to the governmental records, no official change had ever been recorded. I took the necessary steps to have my birth certificate changed, and I am now legally Guy Rice Doud.

I share such detail because there is much in a person's name. I always took special pride in being my grandfather's namesake and felt a certain responsibility that I wouldn't have otherwise. In some way, I felt (and still do) that I had an obligation to all the Rices of the world.

Grandpa was one of those first important molders of dreams in my life, and if it made a difference to him that my middle name was Rice, it makes a difference to me, too.

Grandpa Guy worked for the railroad most of his life, retiring in 1955 after fifty-one years of service. Grandpa had engineered thousands of locomotives westward to the coast along the Northern Pacific railway, and he was always ready with a story about one of his exploits. Before becoming an engineer of diesel trains, he had been a fireman on steam locomotives.

One of his favorite stories detailed stopping the big freight train and chasing wild chickens on the railroad tracks. Once a chicken was caught, Grandpa and the engineer would pluck it and rig up their own special rotisserie. After a few calculated turns of the rotisserie over the train's coal-fired engines, Grandpa and the engineer would have a fine chicken dinner. I remember watching Grandpa's mouth water as he explained to me, while I sat on his lap, just how tasty that chicken was.

Grandpa used to sing "Casey Jones," and I thought he and Casey had been close friends or something. I would sit on Grandpa's lap and listen to him sing or listen to him tell one of his stories, and through the world of imagination, I lived those stories with him.

Grandpa and Grandma resided on the west edge of town, and I spent many days there. Grandma had several large flower gardens, and Grandpa took charge of the tomatoes, potatoes, corn and other vegetables. During the summer months, I would help garden, mow the lawn and do other odd jobs, for which Grandpa provided me with what I thought was more than a generous allowance.

Grandma would always make a first-class dinner, usually roast beef, potatoes, gravy, carrots and apple or mincemeat pie, and I would eat heartily. Before we would eat, Grandma would get out the devotional book, and Grandpa would get out the Bible. As we sat at the table in their kitchen, Grandpa would read the suggested Scripture, and Grandma would read the corresponding lesson from the devotional.

I remember one lesson about sowing and reaping. Grandpa Guy expanded on the lesson, explaining to me that if I wanted to sell sweet corn later that summer, I'd have to do a better job weeding and watering it right now.

The Scripture reading and devotional time would always follow with a short prayer time. Grandpa would often thank God for the rain, the sun, the gifts of life, and Grandma would thank Him for His Son, Jesus, and her family, and for their grandson Guy Rice, who could share the meal and the day with them.

Occasionally a day at Grandpa and Grandma's would involve a trip just north of Staples to Evergreen Hill Cemetery. Grandpa was as particular about the flowers planted at the graves of his parents, Stephen and Fannie Rice, as he and Grandma were about the flowers in their gardens at home.

I can still picture Grandpa on his knees, planting flowers in the gardens at home or in front of his parents' tombstones. Grandpa would begin to grow the flowers while the snow was still on the ground. He would keep the plants in an old shed out back and would shine lights on them to keep them warm and help them grow. The plants would have a home in the shed until the snow was gone and Grandpa was confident no more frosts would come until fall. Then out the plants would come, already well on their way to good growth.

If Grandpa feared a frost after the flowers were transplanted, he and Grandma would cover all the garden plants with blankets and quilts like they were little babies. He would cover the ones at the cemetery, too.

One spring on our way home from Evergreen Hill, Grandpa turned the big green 1954 Buick Special west and drove me out to the spot where he grew up as a boy. Even then as he pointed the landmarks out to me, I realized how important it was to Grandpa—and how important it was to me, too. This is where he had grown up, and what he had experienced and had come to believe was shaping and molding me in no small way.

Often a ride in the Buick would involve a stop at the root beer stand.

"Do you think you have room for a black cow?" Grandpa Guy would ask with a gleam in his eye. He knew my answer. We would finish the floats—Grandpa slurping as much as I—and then head back to what he called "the homestead" to do some more lawn work or gardening.

As I grew older, Grandpa trusted me with more and more responsibility around the homestead. One job I particularly enjoyed was washing and waxing the big Buick Grandpa called "Betty." Bought shortly after I was born, the huge car was in beautiful shape. I liked to help make it shine. It was the only car I ever knew my grandparents to have.

Working with Grandpa, especially weeding the garden, caused me to work up quite an appetite. Although Grandma's dinners should have been sufficient to satisfy anyone's hunger for several days, I was a growing boy, and I always had room for a few of Grandma's cookies.

Grandma knew this. She would call me in for a cookie break mid-afternoon and would bring out her ginger creams. After cookies and milk, Grandpa would be found sitting in the shade by the garage in a spot that just invited the storytelling that would follow.

After a few stories and some bird watching, he would pull out his pocket watch—the one he had used for years on the railroad to make sure his trains were on time—and announce that it was time to get back to work. I have since wondered what would have happened if we had just sat there a bit longer.

Grandpa and Grandma grew old right before my eyes, and I never noticed. Grandma became more and more crippled with rheumatoid arthritis. It got to the point that she could hardly use her hands. She relied more and more on Grandpa to lift her out of the chair and help her get around.

The last time Grandma visited our home for Christmas dinner, I asked her to sing her favorite song so I could record it on the reel-to-reel tape recorder I had received for Christmas.

She sat back in the chair, tilted her head in her odd sort of way, and sang out in a voice obviously once beautiful:

On a hill far away stood an old rugged cross,
The emblem of suffering and shame.

She sang the last verse with such conviction:

Then He'll call me some day to my home far away,
Where His glory forever I'll share.

When she finished, we all sat in silence.

Then she stated, "I want that song sung at my funeral."

And I, who had never been to a funeral, said, "Grandma, you're not going to die."

She just smiled and held my hand with her twisted hand.

I remember a cold February day when Mom picked me up at school. I knew Grandma had been sick, but I hadn't realized how serious it was. The way my mom handled Grandma's death did much to teach me that the faith Grandma had in Jesus was real.

The hardest thing for me was to face Grandpa for the first time.

Mom took me from school out to the homestead. Grandpa sat in his chair, parallel with Grandma's chair. As I entered the living room, Grandpa Guy looked up at me peacefully and held out his big, rough hand.

"Come here, Guy," he said. And he held me for a long time as the tears came.

The funeral was held at the Congregational church where my grandparents had been members for more than fifty years. June Longbella sang "The Old Rugged Cross," and Reverend Olson spoke about Grandma's faith in Jesus.

We sat there, my grandfather, the patriarch, flanked by his daughters and their husbands and grandchildren. I had a new feeling of what it meant to be family.

So many people came up to me to tell me what a fine lady my grandma was and how much she loved her grandchildren. But, of course, I already knew that.

In an outpouring of love and concern, people stopped by the house with hot dishes, Ferny came with her scones, the neighbors brought cakes and pies, and someone shoveled the sidewalk.

Staples seemed to say, "We'll miss your grandma, too."

A couple of months after Grandma's death, we were studying poetry in school. We were assigned to write a poem. A sophomore in Mr. Tomsky's English class, I composed the following verses:

Grandma's Hands

I remember her hands, my grandmother's hands
  All crippled and twisted in pain.
The hands that held children, the hands that baked bread,
  Would never be useful again.

I remember her hands, my Grandma's hands,
All gnarled and painfully bent.
But I saw in those hands a black precious book,
The key to the life that she spent.

I remember her touch, Grandma's touch,
As she grabbed my hand with hers.
With love and tenderness she drew me close,
And whispered these precious words:

"Jesus loves you, always remember,
Jesus loves you, Guy!
Jesus really loves you, son,
He does, and so do I!"

Yes, I remember that voice, Gram's voice,
As one day she read from the book.
She read of His hands, of nails driven through,
Of the pain and suffering He took.

She said, "I look at my hands gnarled in pain,
And sometimes I've questioned why.
But Jesus always answers by taking my hands
And offers a tender reply:

" 'I suffered on Calvary, the spear pierced my side,
The nails were driven by bones.
I suffered and died on Calvary's tree;
I suffered and died alone.

" 'I know your pain; I've felt it too.

15

Believe me, my child, I care.
Just give me your hands and I'll hold yours,
  And help you your burden to bear.'

"I reached for His hands," she said, "as He reached for mine.
  And I felt the holes pierced through.
And my hands, though gnarled, crippled and bent,
  Know no pain like the pain that He knew."

I remember her hands, my Grandmother's hands,
  Folded, as she lay at rest.
And as I touched those hands one last time,
  I thanked God that her life was so blessed.

Those hands that held the Bible, those hands that held me,
  Now hold the Master's hands.
No longer gnarled or twisted in pain,
  They are strong and tender again.

At the bottom of the poem, I wrote, "In memory of a great woman in Christ, Mayme Tooley Rice, by her grandson, Guy Doud."

To be quite honest, I don't remember what grade I received on the poem, but I do know that on the copy I handed in I spelled "gnarled" with a *k* instead of a *g*.

It seemed as though Grandpa had stayed strong and healthy to take care of Grandma, and once she was gone, it was okay for him to act his age, too. Grandpa lived for about a year and a half after Grandma died, but you could tell he longed to be with Christ and with her again.

Grandpa's pocket watch now sits on the mantle of our fireplace, housed in a miniature foot-high grandfather clock. The face of the watch provides the face of the clock. Whenever I look at it, it seems to say that it's about time to do some more weeding, but almost as often it suggests to me that it's time to take a break and have a few ginger creams.

Each spring before Memorial Day, I drive to Evergreen Hill just north of Staples. Sometimes I drive there in my big green 1954 Buick Special that Grandpa left me in his will.

After I've planted the flowers, I stand back and read the tombstone. Grandma picked the verse: "I can do all things through Christ who strengtheneth me" (Phil. 4:13, KJV).

Grandma and Grandpa, you taught me that I can, too. Thanks for being two of the most important molders of my dreams.

Love in a Fold-a-Note

was always more than happy to help. So one day, when my mother's friends were all talking at the same time, one of them stopped to ask: "Could I have another glass of water?"

I overheard the request and with a two-year-old's enthusiasm said, "I get it" and ran off.

"Thank you, dear," said Mom, as I ran down the hall.

Soon I returned with the water.

"Thank you, sweetie; you're a doll," said the lady, although I did spill a little of the water bringing it to her.

"I'd love some water, too," said a lady with big arms.

As I returned with the second and third glasses of water, it finally dawned on my mom. She asked, her voice filled with fear: "Where are you getting the water?"

I wasn't tall enough to reach the sink in the kitchen or the bathroom. (Although on important occasions I had been known to do some clever cupboard climbing to get what I needed.) And I don't think I knew how to work the faucet in the bathtub.

"Oh, no, don't drink any more of the water!" ordered my mother, as her friends stopped with their glasses midair in the journey to their mouths.

Their looks asked "why?" and Mom regretfully obliged: "I think he's getting it out of the toilet." This was something I had been known to do.

I'm not sure—the memory of a two-year-old, you know—but I don't think my mom's friends stayed much longer. I do know that after they left, Mom just held me in her arms and had a touch of a smile as she scolded me.

Someone has written, "Who we are, what we become, depends largely on those who love us." I knew growing up that no one could possibly love me more than my mother.

My earliest memory finds me in my crib. My crib is against the wall, only a few feet from my parents' bed in their small bedroom.

It is night, and I'm awake. I'm frightened and feeling insecure. I want to be held. I want to feel the warmth of human touch. I call my mother. She is asleep there in the bed. My father is asleep as well. I'm frightened of waking my father. I know, though, if my mother hears me, she will understand my fear and comfort me.

I continue to cry, to whimper, to whisper for attention, for reassurance that I'm still loved. I'm reaching through the bars of the crib, trying to reach my mother. Then I feel her hand grasp mine. The touch of love, of reassurance. Her arm, a bridge from bed to crib, her hand enfolding mine. There in the darkness, no words spoken, just a tender touch, and I feel strangely calm.

I knew that hand would always be there for me.

In September 1958 I started school. I remember crying passionately when I discovered that my mother wasn't going to stay in school with me. Although I had to attend school only a half-day every other day, I regarded it as a prison and felt I had received a life sentence.

Getting dressed for school was always a production. I wanted to wear the clothes I usually wore, but Mother insisted I dress up for school. Most of my early school pictures show me with a tie and sweater. But the picture of me that became our family's favorite shows me wearing my Mickey Mouse sweater. My ears stick out almost as far as Mickey's.

Mom came into my bedroom each night, and we would say our evening prayers. She would place a silver dollar over each of my ears. Then she would tape the dollars to my head in an attempt to keep my ears from sticking out.

To this day a debate still rages in my family over whether it worked. Mom insisted that it did, but you can compare my ears with Mickey's and decide for yourself.

Even though I soon learned to accept that I had to go to school, I still looked forward to seeing my mother at the end of each school day. I knew that I would receive a big hug and kiss from her as she would ask, "How was school today, honey?"

As the years passed, I often walked to school with others from my neighborhood. Soon we graduated to riding our bikes. When the weather was bad, Mother would drive me to school and be there at day's end to pick me up.

I remember one late fall day in particular. I rode my bike to school, although the clouds looked heavy and gray. As I pedaled to Lincoln Elementary that morning, tiny flecks of white began to salt my face, coat and gloves. Winter was sending a calling card.

I sat in my classroom, gazing out the window as Minnesota put on its winter premier. My teacher couldn't compete with what was going on outside.

Somehow, even as a child, I knew that Minnesota's four distinct seasons were a special gift from God. They had a way of teaching you about life: spring with life jumping out all around; summer that seemed hot and long, but invited exciting exploration; maple, birch and oak leaves doing a dizzy dance in the fall, sending their colorful notice that another year was almost gone. And then winter—not just winter, but a Minnesota winter. I figured God must love Minnesotans in a special way.

The first snow of the year is always exciting, and this one, as heavy as it was, started me thinking of sleds, snowmen and snowballs, and possible igloo building. I figured that, if it continued like this, school would be canceled the following day, and I would have to shovel. But that would be okay, because I would shovel the snow into a big pile and see if I remembered how to make a snow fort.

I had made some pretty spectacular snow forts, complete with doors and skylights. In the biggest one, I was able to stand with my head barely touching the ceiling.

"Here are some cookies to eat in your snow fort," Mom said, handing me a bag of oatmeal revels with raisins just out of the oven. You couldn't do much in your snow fort, and eating cookies was about as good a thing as I could imagine. All that chewing action was good exercise, and as I sat in my snow fort eating oatmeal revels with raisins, I felt strangely warm.

"What answer do you have, Guy?"

I turned from the window to see my teacher staring at me. This was unfair. She knew I wasn't in the room at that moment. She didn't know, though, that I was warm inside my snow fort eating Mom's oatmeal revel cookies.

I was glad when the day ended and I could go home, but I hadn't brought my boots. Pedaling my old red Schwinn through this stuff was going to be hard. Although we only lived about eight blocks from school, I could have used a snow plow instead of a bike.

But when I came out of school, my bike was gone. I heard a horn honking and turned toward the street. Mom was in our old blue Chevy, my bike sticking out of the trunk. I ran to the car.

"Hi, honey," she said. "Here, put on your boots."

I did, noticing that the boots didn't fit quite as well as they had last winter. Mom had the heater and defroster going full blast, and the windshield wipers labored as they pushed the heavy snow to the sides.

Minnesotans take winter in stride. It may slow us down, but it rarely stops us. With my bike in the trunk and my boots on, it was now business as usual.

On the days Mom picked me up at school, we always stopped to get groceries on the way home. Today was no exception. Heier's Grocery was only a block north of Lincoln Elementary, and we pulled up in front as I finished pulling on my boots.

Heier's was run by Fred and Marie Heier, who were like members of our family. Going to their neighborhood grocery store was like going to a friend's house. They called your name in greeting as you entered their store, and you would call back, "Hi, Fred; hi, Marie."

If someone in our family was sick, Mom would call our order in to Fred, and he would deliver. Sometimes Mom didn't have the money for all the groceries she needed, and Fred would say, "I'll put it on your slip, Jeannette."

All us kids helped Mom find coupons in magazines and newspapers, and Fred and Marie were always patient as Mom counted them out. They were patient, too, as we stood before the meat counter trying to pick out the best cut. Fred would cut your meat any way you wanted it.

Mom got all the ingredients she needed to make my oatmeal revels with raisins at Heier's, and here, too, she got the supplies needed for her annual Christmas baking. Our house was a regular bakery the month between Thanksgiving and Christmas. Mom turned out fudge and peanut brittle, anise candy, date balls, Russian tea cakes, divinity, both white and dark fruit cake, mashed potatoes covered with chocolate that tasted like Mounds candy bars, frosted sugar cookies, lefsa and krumkaka, and what seemed like a hundred other of her specialties.

At Heier's she also bought the cardamom seed to make my favorite Christmas food of all—cardamom bread. Mom used uncracked cardamom seed for the bread.

"The seed that's already cracked isn't as good," she said.

Fred Heier always had uncracked cardamom seed, and although it was expensive, Mom knew that a Christmas without cardamom was like a Minnesota Christmas without snow. I helped Mom crack the peanut-sized seed with a hammer, being careful not to smash the shells too hard.

Cracking the seed was but one small step in making cardamom bread. The entire process had actually begun with the Fourth of July watermelon, when Mom saved the rind to make the citron that she would also use in the bread.

Mom made what seemed like hundreds of loaves of bread. The loaves needed freezing, but when I was young, we didn't have a freezer. In the winter, we didn't need one. Whatever we put in our back porch froze solid. Mom put her boxes of cardamom bread, each loaf wrapped in tinfoil, out in the porch.

Whenever we would finish off a loaf—I prefer mine toasted—I would run out to the porch and quickly grab another silver package. I hated going back to school after the New Year, because not only did that mean Christmas vacation was over, but it also usually meant the cardamom was gone for another year.

We had homemade treats all year round, although the rest of the year didn't offer nearly the variety as Mom's Christmas baking. I know all those sweets certainly contributed to my large stomach.

My mother's stomach was large, too, although its size had little to do with how much she ate.

"Why is your mom's stomach so big?" asked one of my friends, whom I had invited in for some of Mom's Christmas treats. He wasn't being rude. My mother's stomach stuck out like a basketball.

"She has a hernia," I said.

"Can't she get it fixed?"

"I don't think she can," I said.

I knew that because I had asked my mom about her stomach, and she said we couldn't afford the operation. At first her hernia had been quite small, and she had placed silver dollars over it and taped in down, just like she did my ears. But after I was born, it had grown worse and continued to protrude more and more.

I accepted what she said about not being able to afford the operation and didn't stop to wonder how we could afford new Easter clothes for each kid and cardamom bread each Christmas.

I felt I could ask my mother about anything. I remember one morning as I got up for school, I saw Mom sitting and reading a little green book. I had seen her read from this book quite often.

"Whatcha reading?" I asked.

"It's a book called *Twenty-Four Hours a Day,"* she said. "It has little messages in it, meditations and prayers, that help me get through each day."

"Oh," I said. I knew that sometimes I was bad and that sometimes she and Dad had violent arguments, but I hadn't realized she needed help to get through each day.

Mom could see that I was confused.

"Come here, honey," she said, and took me on her lap. "I'm an alcoholic. Do you know what that is?"

"Somebody who drinks a lot of beer and gets drunk all the time?" I couldn't believe that my mom was an alcoholic, because I had never seen alcohol in my house. Some of my friends' parents drank, and I had smelled alcohol, but I had never smelled it on my mom.

Mom explained to me what an alcoholic was, and how, even though she no longer drank, she would be an alcoholic for the rest of her life. Mom told me that she could have never stopped drinking without God and without learning to take life one day at a time. She said that she had almost ruined her life with alcohol and told me that she prayed that I would never drink.

You see, in the late 1930s Jeannette Rice was single and working as a beautician in Brainerd, Minnesota. She had her own beauty shop on Front Street, and things were going well, except that the United States stood on the brink of entering the war in Europe.

Brainerd is only about twenty miles from Camp Ripley, where men from all over America came to be trained. Jeannette met one of those men, and they fell in love.

She brought her soldier home to Staples to introduce him to her mother and father. They were disappointed when Mom told them that she had eloped. Grandma and Grandpa had always hoped for a church wedding, but they were happy for their daughter, who seemed very much in love. Mom showed everyone the wedding ring her soldier had given her, and she wore it with pride.

Within two years, Mom had given birth to two girls, their first children. By this time, the United States had entered the war, and her husband was called into service. Mom longed for the war's end so he could come home and be with her and the girls.

Those were tough years for my mother, raising two children and working full time. Finally the war ended, but her husband never returned.

Mom lived in fear, wondering where he was. Had he been killed and she not notified? Days of painful anxiety were shared by friends and family. Where was he?

The Red Cross finally located my mother's husband, my sisters' father. He had returned from the war. He was not injured. He had not been shot. He was alive and well and living with his wife and children in Missouri.

Further investigation revealed that no wedding license had been filed, no record found of any legal wedding between my mother and this man. The person who had performed the marriage had been a friend of the groom's, and probably wasn't legally able to perform marriages, although my mother never knew it.

She thought she had a husband. She knew her daughters had a father. My mother and my sisters never heard from their husband or father again.

As I listened to Mom tell me about her first husband, I somehow felt that maybe she blamed herself for his never coming back.

Even after marrying my father, Mom still bore much pain. Dad was an alcoholic, too, and though they both had quit drinking, the effects of alcoholism continued to influence their behavior.

But Mom never gave up. Her faith grew. She looked to Christ for strength, and she never quit growing as a person or as a Christian.

In 1960, Patrick Michael was added to our family, and he brought us all great joy. Jan and Nicki loved to play mother to their baby brother, and I, of course, relished my role as older brother.

I remember those as mostly happy years, Mom doing all she could to bring joy and stability to our family. My father had become the assistant chief of police for Staples, and we were proud of our home and family.

After Pat's birth, Mom's hernia grew even worse. It ruptured and engulfed her stomach and her bowels. Gas became locked in the hernia, and she experienced intense pain. She wore a truss most of the time but insisted that since we didn't have any medical insurance we couldn't afford the operation.

Years passed, and finally she had no choice. The pain became so intense that it completely immobilized her. We took her to see our family doctor, Dr. Lund, who ran a battery of tests. The results confirmed our worst fear: Mom had cancer of the colon.

She told us with such courage. When I heard the word "cancer," fear invaded me like a phone call at two in the morning. My folks had celebrated their twenty-fifth wedding anniversary just a few years earlier, and I was planning on their being around for their fiftieth.

Mom had surgery in the fall of 1975. During this time she was a walking testimony to God's power. She kept praying to God to heal her, and she believed He had.

Then Nicki called me early one Sunday in November 1977. Mom and Pat had spent the weekend at Nicki's home in Aitkin, sixty miles east of Staples. Nicki sounded so strong on the phone as she told me that Mom had died in her sleep. Her heart had apparently stopped beating. Nicki suggested that I drive to Staples to be with Dad, who was home alone.

As I spoke with Nicki, I knew that I, too, had to be strong. And yet inside of me a huge part had died. My mind raced with a thousand questions centered on how I could get along without my mother. She had always been there for me. Now she wouldn't be.

I was barely able to see the road through my tears as I drove to Staples to be with my father. I put one of my favorite tapes in my eight-track and sang along:

Shackled by a heavy burden,
'Neath a load of guilt and shame—
Then the hand of Jesus touched me,
And now I am no longer the same.

I remembered the day I had first sung "He Touched Me" at the Congregational church. Wilma Kupitz, the church choir director and youth fellowship advisor, had taught me the song and had accompanied me.

I sang it to my mom as soon as I got home. When I reached the chorus, I could see the tears clouding her eyes.

He touched me, O He touched me,
And O the joy that floods my soul;
Something happened and now I know,
He touched me and made me whole.

"He Touched Me" became my mother's favorite song. It was her testimony put to music. At her funeral a few days later, it was I who sat with the tears clouding my eyes as Mr. and Mrs. Schimmp sang so beautifully: "Something happened, and now I know, He touched me and made me whole."

Jesus certainly had touched her, and she in turn had been healed. Oh, maybe not physically, but Mom was whole.

She had never quit reaching out. Her hand was still there, just as it was that night when I was a child in my crib. I realized God had given me a special mother.

I think I had always realized this, but it became very clear to me when I was a senior at Concordia College in Moorhead, Minnesota. It was 1975, and I was to graduate soon.

"Does your mother write you every day?" a friend asked as we walked away from our mailboxes.

"Yeah, she does," I answered.

"That's incredible," he said.

"Yeah," I said.

Some days she would only write a note, but there was always at least a note. I still have some of the letters Mom sent me. The handwriting on some of them is pretty shaky, because Mom was undergoing chemotherapy, and it made her very sick. But her sickness never kept her from dropping me a note.

Often at the end of her note she would write: "Here's a fiver, buy yourself some pie and coffee. Don't tell Dad."

She didn't want Dad to know she sent me money, because he accused her of being too good to me. And she was.

In many of her notes, Mom would write something like this: "Would sure love to get a letter from you. Dad gets upset when you call home collect, so why not drop a letter, even if it's real short? It would make my day."

I wasn't sure she actually expected me to write. After all, I was a busy college student, and I was a male, and everyone knows how poor men can be about writing.

When Mom asked me why I didn't write, I answered, "I never have any stamps."

One day I went to my post office box and, as usual, Mom had sent a letter. This letter, however, was larger than usual. I opened it. Inside was a blank fold-a-note, bearing a first-class stamp.

She wrote, "Put my address on this note and send it to me with your love. You can't say you don't have a stamp! Love ya loads! Mom."

In 1986, Tammy and I were getting ready to move into a new house. In the process of moving, I was going through all the things I had accumulated through the years. The box I held in my hands was simply marked "College Stuff."

I had transferred it from storage closet to storage closet during my five moves since I had started teaching in Brainerd. I figured the time had finally come to decide what to do with the "stuff" in the box. As I opened it, I discovered it was filled with things from my dorm room at college ten years earlier.

I found odds and ends from drawers, a few notebooks from classes, some pictures of college friends, class schedules, report cards, theater programs, letters from Mom and my sisters, and a blank fold-a-note with a ten-cent stamp.

I held the fold-a-note for a long time. I remembered the day I had received it. "Please send it to me with your love."

I keep the fold-a-note in my Bible. It reminds me of my mother's love that was totally unconditional. It reminds me of Christ's love that is totally unconditional. It reminds me, too, that there are things I need to do today.

Each night as Tammy and I tuck our children in and pray with them, we hold them tight and tell them we love them. Someday when they are on their own, off to college, or tucking in their own children, I hope they are never too busy to take a moment to write our address on a letter and send it to us with their love. Maybe I'll even provide them with self-addressed, stamped fold-a-notes to make it easier for them.

THREE

He Wore a Badge

The light was on!

I felt like a junior policeman whenever I saw the light. It shone from the old Staples water tower behind the fire department and could be seen from almost anywhere in town. I had the responsibility of notifying Dad whenever I saw it.

These were the days before two-way radios had come to Staples, and the light was the signal that a call had come in to the police. Once the police saw the light, they were to contact the dispatcher immediately.

When my father left the railroad, he went to work for the Staples Police Department, and I had become a cop's kid. I felt responsible to help my father enforce the laws.

I ran into the house: "Dad, the light's on!"

My father immediately picked up the telephone and phoned the police operator.

"Yeah, there's a call?"

He listened.

"Yeah, okay, tell her I'll check it out."

"What was it?" I asked, always secretly hoping that maybe someone had robbed a bank and there was going to be a shootout.

"Mrs. Johnson again, complaining that the neighbor's dog keeps going through her garbage."

"Oh." I was obviously disappointed, but I wasn't surprised. Most police calls in Staples weren't the stuff "Dragnet" was made of.

Usually the light meant that a semitrailer truck was at the station next to the city jail and needed to be weighed. It was the policeman's responsibility to weigh them.

I would often ride along with Dad in the police car and talk to the drivers, amazed at their big trucks complete with beds in them.

Once one of the truckers was hauling turkeys. It was only a few weeks before Thanksgiving.

The trucker looked at me and said, "Pick out a turkey."

I didn't know what he meant by "pick out a turkey," but I pointed to one and said, "That one's kind of cute."

Next thing I knew, the trucker had reached into the truck, pulled out the turkey and was shoving it into a gunny sack.

"Here," he said. "Thanksgiving dinner."

He handed me the gunny sack with the turkey gobbling inside.

"What do you say?" Dad asked.

I honestly wasn't sure, but I said, "Thanks."

What did he mean, "Thanksgiving dinner"? This turkey was alive and well and in the gunny sack. You couldn't eat a live turkey.

I didn't have the heart to watch as a few weeks later Dad took "Joe," as I had come to call him, and laid his head across a chopping block. Nor could I help pluck the feathers. Strange though, I didn't have any trouble eating more than my share of turkey dinner.

I rode with Dad in the police car quite often, sitting in the passenger's seat with the shotgun latched to the floor between us and pointed toward the ceiling, readily available should any major riot break out.

As I rode with Dad, I was disappointed that he didn't give out more traffic tickets. The few times he did stop someone, he would usually call the person by name and say something like, "Well, Mabel, we're in kind of a hurry today, aren't we? I think you'd better slow it down, okay?" The warning usually would suffice.

One of the other major responsibilities of a Staples policeman in those days was turning on the street lights. My father, who was the assistant chief on a four-man force, had the evening shift, so this responsibility was usually his. I rode with Dad around town, and we stopped at each light pole that had the switch box to turn on a block or more of lights.

I sometimes wondered why the people living on the block didn't turn on their own lights. If I lived near the pole with the switch, at the first sign of dusk, I would have run outside and flicked the switch.

We lived on Minnesota Highway 210, or Sixth Street, as it was called in Staples, running south out of town. Consequently, our street was one of the first to get the new mercury vapor lights that come on by themselves once it gets dark. Soon the mercury lights replaced all the lights with switches, just as the two-way radio made the light on the water tower obsolete.

Occasionally, though, I have a dream. In my dream the light on the water tower is blinking. *Blinking!* I've never seen it blink before. This must be a call of great urgency!

I rush into the house and tell my father. He puts down his corn on the cob and immediately rings the police dispatcher.

Some escaped murderers from Stillwater prison are headed toward Staples! They're being chased by highway patrolman Floyd Wise, who has spotted their stolen car near Park Rapids. Shots have been exchanged, and Floyd's cruiser has taken some direct hits.

Dad jumps into Staples's squad car and rushes to the west of town to head off the criminals. Soon their car is screaming into town, and they're firing at anyone who gets in their way. The robbers see that the Staples police have erected a roadblock. They turn north on one of Staples's side streets, taking the corner on two wheels and smashing into a telephone pole. They quickly abandon their car and set off on foot into a swamp with tall grass, firing shots as they flee.

Local law enforcement officials surround the field. Who will follow them into the swamp to capture them?

Dad doesn't think twice. He unbolts the shotgun between the seats of the police car, checking to make sure it's loaded. He heads out into the swamp. It's tough going in the tall grass. He stops. He fires a shot above the grass as a warning.

And then he yells, "You'd better come out!"

Nothing happens. He continues into the swamp.

Suddenly, he is on them in the grass. These convicted murderers have nothing to lose by killing someone else. They have their guns pointed at Dad. He lowers his shotgun.

"You can shoot me, but that just means someone else is going to shoot you. Give it up."

There is a moment's hesitation. Finally, they drop their pistols and surrender.

Dad follows behind them, his shotgun leveled at their backs, as they come out of the swamp with their hands raised.

This is a dream, but except for a few minor details like the light on the water tower blinking, the incident actually took place. On July 13, 1972, my dad and Bud Trana walked out into a swamp at the northwest end of Staples and captured two escaped murderers from Stillwater Prison. The governor issued citations for bravery to my father, Bud Trana and highway trooper Floyd Wise.

As it happened, I was away at Parker Scout Reservation on North

Long Lake near Merrifield, Minnesota. I was an assistant Scoutmaster for Staples Troop 61, and we were halfway through our week at camp.

One of the adults from a nearby campsite who had been listening to the radio came by because he knew that we, being from Staples, would probably be interested in what was going on at home.

He told us what he had heard: "The Staples police captured these escaped criminals, and I guess there was quite a shootout. Yeah, I guess one of the policeman was killed."

With my heart in my throat I ran to the headquarters building and called home. I was never so happy to hear my father's voice.

Dad explained everything that happened in a calm, easy way. I formed the picture in my mind of my father walking bravely into the swamp, knowing quite well that he could be shot. I could see him as he came on the convicts in the grass. I could see him leveling the shotgun at their heads. I was proud.

I couldn't believe he had actually used the shotgun from the police car. I remembered only one other time Dad used the shotgun.

One dark summer night Dad was working the late shift. He swung by our house when I was just getting ready to go to bed. "You want to shoot some rats?" he asked.

"Sure," I said. I had never shot rats before and wondered where one went to do such a thing. I wondered if a host of rats had invaded Staples and if the responsibility of rat elimination had also been given to the Staples police.

"Where are we going to shoot rats?" I inquired, wondering if I could add "rat eliminator" to my resume after "junior policeman."

"Out at the dump," Dad said.

The Staples City dump has since gone the way of the light on the water tower and street lights with off and on switches, but when I was a kid, a trip to the dump was a highlight of the week. It sounds rather crude, but it was always interesting to see what other families in town threw away. Once in a while something was worth saving, something that deserved a second chance at life.

But from what I'd heard, the dump wasn't a place you wanted to go to at night. It was spookier than a cemetery, because at night the rats came out to take their turn checking out everyone's garbage.

Dad and I drove to the dump, which was only about five blocks east of our house. One of the advantages of going to the dump in the police car was that we could use the spotlight on the side of the car to search out those beady little rat eyes. We shot the rats right from the car; there was no need to get out, for which I was grateful.

Once we had a rat in the spotlight, Dad used the shotgun and I used his police revolver. He explained that it was a good idea to fire a gun every once in a while, just to make sure it was still in operating order.

As I listened to Dad explain about capturing the convicts from Stillwater, I couldn't help but think of him walking into the swamp with the same shotgun we had used to blast rats.

When he told about walking up to the two men where they lay in the grass, he suddenly got very serious: "I still don't know why they didn't shoot me."

" 'Cuz we still need you, Dad." At that moment, I realized how much I loved my father.

Despite the memories of turning on streetlights and shooting rats, I had always longed for my dad to be more involved in my life. I knew that I loved him, but I wasn't always sure that he loved me. He had a tremendously difficult time expressing feelings, and it wasn't until years later that I began to realize he needed the same thing I did: he needed love. Maybe he was unable to give me the attention I felt I needed, because he had never been given attention himself.

My father, Jesse Frank Doud, was the only boy in a family of seven growing up during the depression. His father was an alcoholic. Jesse quit school in the eighth grade to help support the family. He got married at seventeen, and had his son James at the age of eighteen.

When the war came, my father joined the 82nd Airborne and was one of fifty thousand Allied soldiers who took part in trying to take the Anzio beachhead thirty-three miles south of Rome. It was a very costly battle for the Allies.

Before the jump, the paratroopers were told to write a letter home, and each knew it could very well be the last letter he would write. My father survived the jump, but his legs were filled with shrapnel. He was captured by the Nazis and was forced to march north to a stalag, where he remained imprisoned for fifteen months until he was liberated.

I've tried to put myself in my father's shoes. I'm eighteen. I'm told there is a good chance I will not survive the jump in the morning. My commanding officer suggests that tonight it would be a good idea to write to those we love. I sit down to write a letter, but what do I write: "I don't want to die"?

I rarely heard my dad talk of his war experiences. What I know I have learned mostly from what others have told me. I know so few things about my father's past, and yet I realize that his past—in no small way—affects my future.

I did know that my father was wounded and imprisoned in a stalag during the war. I had watched "Hogan's Heroes" on television, but I knew the stalag my father was in was nothing like Stalag 13, and the commandant no Colonel Klink.

One of the rare times he talked about the war, he spoke of all the young men, his friends, who had been killed. And then he stared out into space and said in a monotone: "I don't know why I survived."

When he said that, I didn't know how to answer him. I don't think he expected an answer. Years later, after capturing the escaped convicts, he wondered again why he hadn't been killed. I knew how to answer him then.

Dad returned home from World War II on a Danish hospital ship, but for him another war needed to be fought. Soon his first marriage ended in divorce. His second child, Ronald, died of spinal meningitis at the age of eight. One Fourth of July, two of my father's sisters drowned, one trying to save the other. For my father, life seemed to consist of one tragedy after another. How was he to cope?

Children of alcoholic parents are known to have a greater propensity for alcoholism, and so it is not surprising that booze became my father's best friend.

My father met Jeannette Rice, who had also known her share of personal tragedy and who also looked to alcohol to help her survive. One New Year's Eve, Jeannette and Jess decided to elope. They woke up a Justice of the Peace, who performed their marriage ceremony on the spot.

Jeannette realized alcohol was destroying their lives and their family. She began to attend Alcoholics Anonymous, quit drinking and prayed that Jess might quit drinking, too.

But my dad failed to recognize he had a serious problem. He bragged that he had been in "every jail from Minnesota to Texas." Drinking was like a right arm; it was difficult to conceive of getting along without it.

Mom resorted to all sorts of measures. She pleaded. She got angry. She threw his bottles away. But the drinking continued.

Finally he quit drinking. One of the things I don't know about my father is what happened to make him stop. He talked of "reaching the bottom." He said that if he had continued drinking, he probably wouldn't have lived another year.

He began to attend Alcoholics Anonymous with my mother, and along with her, he remained sober for the rest of his life. Yet my dad admitted that not a day passed without his thirsting for a drink.

Unfortunately, somewhere along the way, Dad quit going to A.A. He may have quit drinking, but he hadn't replaced the drinking with anything constructive. The same feelings that had caused him to drink were repressed, but they surfaced in irrational ways.

Some therapists refer to this behavior as a "dry drunk." My sisters, my brother and I remember violent outbursts of temper—my father slamming the door and leaving for days at a time, with us left at home to wonder if he would return.

I understand all of this now. It wasn't that my father didn't love me. I'm convinced now that the love I received from him was the best he knew how to give. His alcoholism, strange silences, violent temper, inability to express constructive feelings, are more easily understood in light of the circumstances of his past. But it's difficult to explain these things to a child.

I fondly remember the times Dad and I did spend together. We did simple things. I loved playing baseball and softball, and I marveled how my dad could throw a curve ball.

Someone would later tell me that my father played on a softball team from Grand Forks, North Dakota, just across the border from where he had grown up in East Grand Forks, Minnesota. My dad's team won the North Dakota State Championship and went to the Fast Pitch Softball World Series at Soldier Field in Chicago.

I saw a picture of my dad in his baseball uniform once. The picture was taken at Soldier Field. He was a young man of about twenty. He had jet black hair and stood about five feet nine inches. There was fire in his eyes.

He was the catcher on the team. You played injured or not, because only ten men from Grand Forks traveled to Chicago. My father broke a finger catching a fast ball. He taped it and kept playing. He struck out once and hit three home runs.

I inherited my father's love for the game. When I was a young boy, the Washington Senators became the Minnesota Twins, and I became an avid fan. A dream of mine was to attend a game. We didn't have a car that could make it the 130-some miles to Metropolitan Stadium in Bloomington, but my dad knew how badly I wanted to go to a Twins' game.

Hjalmer Randgaard's car could make it to Bloomington and back, and so Dad arranged for us to go with Hjalmer.

Whenever Dad received a silver dollar, he would put it in an old sock in his dresser drawer among his underwear. This was the only savings I remember my parents having. On very special occasions, Dad would take some silver dollars out of the sock. He went to the sock now to help finance our trip to Metropolitan Stadium.

It was one of the greatest days of my life. We watched Harmon Killebrew, Bob Allison, Tony Oliva and Earl Battey, my heroes! Dad used a silver dollar to buy me a souvenir program, and I used it to memorize the batting averages and other statistics of my favorite players.

I wore a pair of green socks to the game that day, and when I got home, I took them off and hid them under my mattress because they were the socks I had worn to the Twins' game. I vowed I would never wear them again.

I don't know whatever happened to those socks.

Another day that stands out in my memories of my father was a day when I was about seven years old. I was swimming at Jakey's, a local swimming hole on the Crow Wing River. Mom and Dad were sitting on the bank, watching me.

I stepped into a drop-off. The water was over my head. The current was taking me down. I couldn't swim. I knew I was going to die. I struggled. My struggling only seemed to make matters worse. Soon I was going down for the third time. And suddenly, Dad was there.

He had jumped into the river, clothes and all, and his strong arms were carrying me to shore, lifting me above the fast current.

I buried my head in his shoulder, sobbing with fear, yet secure that I was in my father's arms.

One hot day during the summer of 1989, Tammy and the kids and I decided to go swimming. We drove out to Jakey's. The Crow Wing wasn't as fast or as deep as I remembered it, just as the sliding hill behind my boyhood home isn't nearly as steep as it once was.

Soon the entire Doud family was splashing in the river. In its shallowest spots, the river came up only to the toes of two-year-old Jessica, and she was content to sit in the shallows on the sandy bottom with the river diverging around her. Seth and Luke, feeling more adventurous, wandered out farther toward the middle. I warned them about the drop-off near the old concrete foundation.

Despite my warnings, Luke stepped into the drop-off and suddenly was under water. I was only a few feet away from him and pulled him up before he had a chance to become too frightened, but he was still shaking and crying, and he clutched me tightly as I carried him to shore.

I wonder if Luke will remember that experience like I remember the experience with my Dad at Jakey's. I felt so secure in my father's arms, finding such strength from his strength.

I guess I felt that my father would always be strong and invincible, so when he suffered a heart attack my freshman year in college, I started to do a lot of thinking. My parents weren't immortal. Just as Grandma and Grandpa had both died, my parents would also die. I believed death was victory for a Christian, but my father—by his own admission—wasn't a Christian.

One night I sat listening to Bill, the adviser for our InterVarsity Christian Fellowship Group. He was speaking about witnessing.

I can still hear his voice clearly: "It's often most difficult to witness to those you're closest to—like a mom or a dad."

"Like a dad . . ." At IVCF that Thursday evening, I asked God to send someone to witness to my father about Jesus. I secretly wished that Bill could talk to him.

God soon answered my prayer, and He sent someone I thought was totally wrong for the job—me.

I prayed for hours before I walked into the room where my father sat smoking a cigar and watching television. I walked over and turned the TV off right in the middle of whatever program he was watching.

"I need to talk to you, Dad." I had never said that before.

He looked at me and said, "What is it, Sonny?"

He always called me "Sonny," or "Yonny," and I've never known why.

Then he saw how serious I was. "Are you in some kind of trouble?"

I felt that if I had been, somehow Dad would have jumped into the strong current and saved me.

"Dad, the other night you said you weren't a Christian."

"Oh," said Dad, as he figured out what the topic of discussion was going to be.

A few nights before, I had invited Dad to a Bible study. We had read from Acts 11:26: "The disciples were called Christians first at Antioch."

Dad had asked: "What's a Christian?"

The group fell silent. I finally answered: "When we were reading the second chapter of Acts, someone asked Peter what one had to do to be a Christian."

I turned to Acts 2:38 and asked everyone to turn with me. "Repent and be baptized, every one of you, in the name of Jesus Christ for the forgiveness of your sins. And you will receive the gift of the Holy Spirit."

I concluded: "A Christian is someone who believes in Jesus, repents of sin, is baptized and receives the Holy Spirit."

My father shocked everyone: "Well, then, I guess I'm not a Christian."

I was unprepared to talk to Dad in front of all the other people in our neighborhood group, but now, alone, I had to.

"Why aren't you a Christian?"

"Oh, I believe in God. I believe in Jesus, but I've never really repented or been baptized."

"Why not?"

"I've done too many bad things, Sonny. I don't think God can forgive me."

"There is no sin God can't forgive, Dad, except the sin of never wanting to be forgiven."

I prayed with my dad that night to receive Jesus Christ as his Savior. He had been rejecting a Jesus that I didn't believe in either, a Jesus who doesn't forgive and doesn't forget.

I didn't sleep a wink that night, realizing that the name "Jesse Frank Doud" had been added to the Lamb's Book of Life.

In early 1980, another monumental experience took place for my father. I invited him to supper at my house to meet Tammy's mother, Ruth. Tammy and I were to be married in June, and we thought Jesse and Ruth should meet.

Whatever chemistry existed between Tammy and me also existed between Jesse and Ruth. They hit it off.

Tammy and I were wed in June as planned, and our folks stood up with us. Then, in August, we stood up with them, as they stood before the same altar where we had given our vows.

People find it interesting to note that my father was my father-in-law; my mother-in-law is my stepmother; my wife is my stepsister; and our children are our niece and nephews.

When, in the spring of 1985, I was selected as the Brainerd, Minnesota, Teacher of the Year, my father was happier than I was. I hadn't seen him for several months because he and Ruth had spent the winter in Tucson. But now that the worst of winter was over, they, like many "snow birds," had returned to Minnesota.

During the winter, Dad had been hospitalized at the Veterans Hospital in Arizona. His heart, having suffered several more attacks, had enlarged considerably and was so weak the doctors said he was not a candidate for surgery. The circulation in his legs had become poor, and Dad was having a difficult time getting around.

So I was happy when Dad and Ruth drove over from Staples to go to church on Palm Sunday with Tammy, Seth, Luke and me. After church, Dad and Ruth came to the house for dinner. Dad spent several hours that afternoon looking through the portfolio I had assembled to enter the Minnesota Teacher of the Year Program. The portfolio was filled with letters of recommendation, news stories, pictures and my written philosophy of education.

I think Dad read every word in the portfolio. He kept shaking his head and saying, "I'm proud of you, boy, I'm so proud of you."

When he and Ruth stood to leave, he turned to me, embraced me and then did something he had never done before—he kissed me on the lips. My first reaction was to turn away so his kiss would fall on my cheek. But I didn't. We kissed.

With tears in his eyes, he said again, "I'm so proud of you."

As he slowly limped to the car, I stood crying.

Right before he got into the car, he turned and said, "See you Wednesday."

"See you Wednesday, Dad," I called back.

Wednesday the local teachers' association had planned a reception at the high school to honor my selection as Teacher of the Year.

The next morning, someone knocked on my classroom door. It

was Stu Lade, a fellow teacher. "Guy, you have a phone call."

I hate phone calls that interrupt my class, so I said, "Can you take a message?"

"It's your mother."

I walked into the English Resource Center. Somehow I knew what she was going to say.

"Guy, Jess died about an hour ago. He was in the bathroom, and I heard a loud thump. I ran in, and there he was. The doctor says he thinks he died before he hit the floor."

At the funeral home later that day, it was decided that I would give my father's eulogy. As I helped make the funeral arrangements, Joe Brenny, the mortician, asked me, "Would you like to see your father?"

Seeing my father's corpse would help the reality of death come sooner. We entered the embalming room, and I saw his body lying on the table, covered by a sheet up to his neck. Those lips were the ones that had kissed me the day before and spoke words of pride. Now they looked cold and tight.

"Do you have anything you wished you had said to your father?" Joe asked.

I stared at my dad, asking Joe's question of myself. "No, I don't. Everything I ever wanted to say to him, I did."

"You're very fortunate," Joe replied.

From where I sit typing now, my father's policeman's hat and night stick are just an arm's reach away. My dad always took great pride in his uniform. His shoes were polished mirrorlike. His hat, though, he tilted to the side, in his own cocky way. The badge on the front of the hat is that of the Staples Police Department. On the side of the hat are my father's paratrooper wings. The eighteen-year-old boy who jumped at Anzio displayed great courage but not as much courage as the middle-aged man who wasn't afraid to learn to love.

Not too long ago, a stranger came up to me on the street. "Are you Jess Doud's boy?"

"Yes," I was proud to respond.

"You know, your dad was one of the best softball players I ever knew. And he could do one-handed push-ups all day long."

"How did you know my dad?"

"We grew up together. We were in A.A. together. We were members of the same club; both a couple of drunks. But your dad, he was a brave man."

I wondered if my dad's boyhood friend knew how brave.

The old Staples water tower has been torn down, the police beacon light long since gone. But I can close my eyes and see my dad. And when I see him, I yell, "Dad, the light's on!"

What I Learned in School (That They Never Knew They Taught Me)

Danny drooled. It was a perpetual problem with him. He would flap his arms and get so excited when he talked that sometimes he would splash you with his drool. I learned my lesson soon and always tried to stay out of his range.

Some of our classmates were less than kind to Danny and were quick to point at his drool and yell, "Gross! Gross!" They did this so frequently that whenever anyone saw Danny, he or she would just point at him and yell, "Gross! Gross!" whether Danny was drooling at the moment or not.

Danny seemed to like to be kidded. The more attention he got, the more he appeared to like it.

One winter day at recess out behind Lincoln Elementary, Danny had a particularly bad case of the drools. And it was an especially cold day.

Usually on very cold days we stayed inside the school, but as I look back, every once in a while the teacher made us go outside no matter how cold it was. I think she needed the break and hoped that maybe the arctic air would help cool us off.

Even though we had been outside for what seemed like less than a minute, Danny's drool froze, forming an icicle that extended about half an inch below his chin.

I think I was the first one to notice the icicle, but I didn't say anything about it, because I didn't know if Danny knew he was wearing an icicle, and I didn't want to embarrass him.

I guess I should have told him that he had a frozen drool icicle hanging from his face, because when Marty found out, he notified the entire student body: "Gross! Gross! Super, super gross!" he yelled. "Look at Danny! His drool is frozen! Gross! Gross!"

We were all used to Danny drooling, but we had never seen his drool freeze before, so this was a special event. Danny, however, didn't seem to react noticeably to the extra attention. With his fingers sticking through the mitten of his right hand, he simply reached up to the left side of his mouth to feel his icicle. Not everyone has his own personal icicle.

Danny felt his for a minute, and then he gently broke it off. Then he turned and looked at Carol. I don't know why he picked Carol. Maybe it was because she was taller than anybody else, or maybe it was because she was yelling louder than anybody else.

For whatever reason, Danny lowered his little icicle as if it were a spear, and charged like Don Quixote toward Carol, who stood tall and erect, appearing more formidable than any windmill.

When Carol saw that Danny intended to stab her with his icicle, she set a Lincoln Elementary School track record, which I believe is still on the books today. Danny did a pretty good job of catching up to her, though, as the rest of us yelled, "Get her, Danny, get her!"

If recess had been just a bit longer, I think Danny might have caught her. Unfortunately our teacher was blowing her whistle, our signal that recess was over, and we needed to get back to the serious studies of the afternoon.

I don't think that recess had the effect the teacher had planned, because we were even more animated after recess than we had been before. The teacher couldn't figure out why. None of us told her about Danny's icicle. There are some things, after all, that teachers just don't need to know.

Almost every one of us kids who was at recess that day graduated from Staples High School in 1971. In Staples, almost no one ever drops out of school, and few people move away.

But Danny did. He and his family moved after sixth grade. They moved to a bigger town and a bigger school, although Danny's grandparents stayed in Staples.

The year we all graduated without Danny, an article appeared in the *Staples World* about him. (In the *Staples World* you could find lots of interesting news. I especially liked the local items from surrounding communities that told you who had coffee at whose house and stuff like that.)

But the article I'm remembering reported that Danny, who was the grandson of Staples residents, had graduated from his school as the valedictorian and had enlisted in the Marines. He was a member of the Special Forces, a Green Beret, and was being sent to Vietnam.

In the spring, right before we graduated, Carol won a medal at the state track meet. That was written up in the *Staples World,* too.

I always liked Danny. I never kidded him, no matter how bad his drooling got. I didn't like kidding, or being made "fun of." I never ridiculed anyone, maybe because I knew too well the pain of being teased.

One day, it was as if someone turned on a light and said: "You are fat and consequently worthy of ridicule."

I was learning a lot more in school than they realized they were teaching me. The most significant lessons had nothing to do with reading or writing or arithmetic, but rather, I was learning about me, about who I was, and whether or not that was good.

Show-and-Tell time was a perfect example of this. I remember some marvelous moments from Show and Tell.

Johnny, who had been out of school for a week, figured his classmates should know why, so he brought his tonsils to class in a jar and accidentally dropped and broke it. The assignment one Tuesday was to bring a picture of your pet, if you had one. Mark decided to actually bring his pet. He brought a pig named Olly and told the class his house was filled with them. Mary said she wanted to show the class how to make an egg go into a bottle. Her father had helped her with this at home. After three broken eggs and no success, Mary began to cry and said: "My dad can do it."

I remember those experiences and others. I listened and watched my classmates during Show and Tell. As I did, I compared myself to them.

Bill showed pictures of his trip to Disneyland and Knott's Berry Farm and told how this coming summer his family was going to Alaska. Rachel had her own horse, and she brought some brushes and a blanket and explained proper horse grooming. Linda was learning to play the ukulele and demonstrated her progress, accompanying herself as she sang "Red River Valley." Paul brought pictures of all the deer and trophy fish caught by his father, grandfather, brothers and relatives. The fish were all caught at their lake cabin near Walker, Minnesota, where they spent the summer.

As I listened to Bill, I thought about taking trips. Our car wasn't very reliable. The tires were bald, and the muffler needed replacing. You could break off pieces of the car around the tire wells, which were rusted from the road salt of ten Minnesota winters.

I was sure I would never get to Disneyland or Knott's Berry Farm, but I was hoping we could go to The Paul Bunyan Amusement Center in Brainerd, thirty miles away. I heard that Paul, the world's largest animated talking man, raised his arm as you entered the grounds and called you by name.

I could hear Paul: "And there's Guy Doud, from Staples."

Once Paul's arm was raised, he would say, "There's a big 'hi' for ya!"

I knew that at Disneyland, Mickey Mouse and Donald Duck didn't know your names.

As I listened to Rachel, I thought about pets. Our pet was a dog named Mugsy, and he never required much grooming. But one day Mugsy decided to run out in the street. It was as if he decided he had had enough, and he ran right out in front of an oncoming car.

We buried him in the backyard, and someone said something about "doggy heaven," but I wasn't so sure. I soon began to lobby for a new pet.

We had a canary, too, but the door on his cage was left open, and he flew right out of his cage and out the front door into the rest of the world. I couldn't say I blamed him.

We had another bird, too, named Chip. Chip could actually talk. But I don't think he liked cages either, and we found him dead one morning on his cage floor. We buried him out back, near Mugsy, but no one said anything about a heaven for birds.

Linda was playing her ukulele. As I listened, I thought about musical instruments and music. I tried to play a ukulele once, but the ukulele I had couldn't play several chords, and my fingers had better things to do.

Linda sang:

> *From this valley they say you are going,*
> *We will miss your bright eyes and sweet smile,*

For they say you are taking the sunshine
That brightens our pathway awhile.

I wondered who was going, why they were going and where they were going. When she reached the chorus, I almost felt like I should go up and sit by her. Actually I would have liked to sing along with her.

I had a nice voice. My grandma and my mom were always telling me what a beautiful voice I had. Whenever we sang in class, I sang louder than everybody else because I wanted everyone to hear my voice, hoping one of my classmates would notice my voice and say, "Listen to Guy; isn't that beautiful?" Instead, the teacher looked at me and said, "Guy, don't sing so loud, please."

As Paul showed pictures of his family's gutted deer, and pictures of the fish caught at their lake cabin, I thought about hunting and how wonderful it must be to have a lake cabin to retreat to in the summer.

As for the hunting part of it, I had shot a few rats, but I had never been hunting for anything you actually ate. I remembered my grandpa telling about the only time he went deer hunting. He had a giant buck in his sights, and he could see the deer's big brown eyes staring right at him. Grandpa began to squeeze the trigger, but he froze. He couldn't kill it. It was looking right at him.

"Big brown eyes," Grandpa said.

Maybe if it hadn't been looking at him, he could have squeezed the trigger and had a trophy rack for his wall, but those big brown eyes haunted him. Besides, this deer was someone's dad, and he didn't have the heart to break up a family. Grandpa decided he would never go hunting again.

Although I secretly envied Paul's hunting trips, I decided I wouldn't be able to shoot a deer either. But when Paul talked about fishing and pulled out the pictures of his fish, that was something else again.

I was boldly jealous. I loved fishing, although I had been fishing only once, in a little stream a block south of our house.

Late one summer afternoon when I was about nine, I grabbed the fishing pole from our back porch. I had never seen anyone use this fishing pole, and I wasn't sure it knew how to catch fish. I dug up some worms that were just waiting to go fishing, and off we went to the stream. I couldn't believe how easy it was. A fish in that stream immediately grabbed my worm. That fish put up quite a fight, too, but I reeled him in.

The fish was ugly-looking with a mustache, but I was proud of him. I thought if I quickly got him home, maybe Mom could prepare him for supper.

Moments later, out of breath, I was showing Mom my fish.

She said, "It's a nice fish, honey, but it's a bullhead, and you can't eat bullheads."

Dad said, "I know some people who smoke bullheads, but yours is too small."

It looked pretty big to me. I wished I had a picture of my fish to show Paul.

Show and Tell taught me those things and much more. I'm sure the teacher never knew that as I listened to the other students, I sometimes wished I could do what they did. Sometimes I even wished I could be them.

Dress-Up Day is another time when school teaches us lessons we would rather not learn. On Lincoln's Dress-Up Day, Clarence wore a rust-colored, polyester leisure suit and a blue tie so wide you could have made a flag out of it. His boots wore their Sunday polish, and his trousers were held in place by a belt with a buckle that looked like a little shield protecting his stomach.

That must have been Clarence's Easter outfit from a few years back, because the pants' cuffs didn't quite reach the tops of his boots. You could see the white socks between the boots and the trousers, and just a little bit of his leg. But I think Clarence thought he looked nice, and I was disappointed when even Danny joined in teasing him.

Of all the revelations in school, one of the most startling is when you finally figure out how smart you are. No one actually comes right out and says: "You're smart," or "You over there in the green shirt and purple pants, you're dumb," but in a way it might be easier if they would. It would save lots of time trying to figure it out.

You wouldn't have to compare the comments on your paper with the comments on your neighbor's, and you wouldn't wonder why Sally's pictures were always the ones the teacher showed the class.

I think I lost it when we started on negative numbers. I was pretty good at adding, subtracting, multiplying and dividing, but square roots and negative numbers. . .

What I really hated was when they started mixing up math with English. I had a difficult enough time with numbers alone, but then, one day the teacher started adding x's and y's, and then she squared them besides. I couldn't figure out how you could square a letter of the alphabet.

I got one of my papers back, and on it the teacher had used a can of red paint and underlined my failing grade so many times that I realized not only wasn't I any good at math—I just wasn't any good. Then the teacher told the class that Linda had a perfect paper, and I knew that the teacher liked Linda.

A few years later, Linda sat in front of our art class in junior high school, holding a guitar as if she were ready to sing "Red River Valley" again. But our teacher wasn't interested in her singing or her guitar-playing progress, our art teacher was interested in drawing. The assignment was to do a chalk drawing of Linda.

I picked out the colors with care. They had to match the colors of Linda and her guitar, and I wanted even the color of the folding chair to be perfect. I spent twenty minutes finding the right color for her eyes that were such a gentle and pretty brown.

Although I was happy to draw Linda, I figured if I were allowed to draw any picture I wanted, I would draw the deer my grandpa could have shot. I would use the same brown for the deer's eyes as I was using for Linda's.

Drawing Linda was even more difficult than picking out the right colors. How do you make a hand so that it holds the neck of a guitar? And how do you keep the fingers from looking like a pancake? I used a black felt-tip pen to aid in separating the fingers one from another.

I also used the pen to create the pupils of Linda's eyes. By the time I was finished, I think Linda's eyes got mixed up with the deer's eyes. When you looked at my drawing, Linda's eyes looked right at you as if they were saying, "How can you shoot me? I have a family to take care of."

Regardless, I was pretty proud of my chalk drawing and was very unhappy when the teacher gave me a $D+$ and wrote: "You need to work on getting things in proportion."

I took Linda and her guitar home and explained to Mom about her eyes. Mom thought the drawing was very good and suggested I put it up out in the porch and even gave me a couple of thumb tacks to pin it to the wall. Before I tacked Linda to the wall, I turned her over and drew a little line through the middle of the D and felt that a $B+$ was a respectable grade for my efforts.

Linda and her guitar hung on the wall in our back porch, her eyes staring at you, pleading for life. It hung there until we were going to have an auction after my parents died.

As we were getting ready for the auction, I took Linda down and figured I would bring her home to Brainerd, thinking that I could put her up on the wall in our garage. But as I looked at her, I could see that somehow the chalk in her eyes had become smudged, and the black felt tip separating her fingers had faded, leaving her hands looking like pancakes on her guitar strings. So I threw the picture in the trash.

As I tossed Linda into the trash, it was hard to say goodbye, because I could still see her back in Lincoln Elementary, her ukulele on her lap, singing with such compassion:

Come and sit by my side if you love me,
Do not hasten to bid me adieu,
But remember the Red River Valley
And the girl that has loved you so true.

What Linda didn't know is that I kind of had a crush on her. That was one of the reasons I had taken such great efforts to make sure my chalk drawing of her was the best that I could do.

Linda was nice to me; she never made fun of me, and I thought that maybe she liked me, too. She would smile at me, and I would feel warm all over.

FIVE

Guy Isn't Going to Make It, Is He?

I lost myself at the movies. I especially loved nature movies set in the mountains, because there aren't any mountains close to Staples, except, of course, the mountains of snow the Street Department makes each winter.

At the movies, I could command a submarine and go far into the ocean depths. As the enemy destroyer cruised above, I held my breath, hoping he wouldn't detect us. Once he passed, we would come up off the bottom. I would find him through the periscope, and then I would give the order, "Fire one!" and we would send the first torpedo quickly on its way toward the destroyer.

I had given permission to one of my men to paint an evil red grin on the torpedo. (Although you couldn't see it because the film was in black and white.)

Then, again looking through the periscope, charting the course of the first torpedo, I'd yell, "Fire two! Fire three!" and I'd watch as all three torpedoes, with their colorful smiles, blew the destroyer out of the water.

I could afford to go to the movies because admission was fifty cents, and I always had at least that much from my paper route and from the money Grandpa paid me for helping out at the homestead. I had extra money for popcorn, pop and candy, too, because they went with a movie like ice cream went with apple pie. I wouldn't think of one without the other.

I would pay an extra nickel to get a few more squirts of butter, and once satisfied that my popcorn was adequately saturated, I would always sit in exactly the same spot in the theater, just like Grandpa and Grandma always sat in the same pew at church. Once situated with my popcorn, pop and Milky Ways, I was ready for an adventure.

"Hi, Guy," she said, and I looked up. There was Linda. She was entering the row right in front of me and had noticed me sitting there. She was kind enough to greet me. Linda didn't have her ukulele or her guitar, she had her boyfriend on her arm. He didn't bother to say "hi" to me.

"Hi, Linda. You gonna watch the movie?" I asked.

Linda's boyfriend, Sam, just turned and looked at me, and it seemed as though he were staring at my popcorn and Milky Ways.

"Got enough to eat?" he asked.

I didn't answer him but laughed, giving him the benefit of the doubt and wishing I hadn't asked Linda if she was going to watch the movie.

I laughed at the cartoons but wished that just once the coyote would catch up to the roadrunner. What I couldn't figure out was how the coyote could afford all the elaborate devices he used to try to catch the roadrunner. If he had so much money, why didn't he just go out and buy himself a first-class meal? But then I figured that the roadrunner was one of those things money couldn't buy, and the coyote wanted to catch him not so much because he was hungry, but because the roadrunner was a challenge, like a mountain just waiting to be climbed, or an enemy destroyer needing to be sunk.

Not long after the movie started, Sam put his arm around Linda. She didn't seem to mind. I tried not to look, but I couldn't help it, and I watched as he gently rubbed her neck. As he rubbed, my popcorn seemed to disappear more quickly. I put down the popcorn to have a Milky Way, and when I had finished it, I used the toothpick from my Swiss knife to get the caramel out from between my teeth.

As I picked my teeth, I decided Linda was too good for Sam and that she deserved someone better, someone who would stand up with her as she played her guitar. Someone who also had a beautiful voice and could sing with lots of volume.

The movie ended. It hadn't been the adventure I had expected. I always liked to stay to watch the credits, but Sam and Linda got up before it even said "The End."

So I gathered two Milky Way wrappers, the empty, family-sized butter barrel, and the cup the pop had been in. I didn't like leaving my garbage on the floor.

Sam looked at me as I stood to leave, garbage in both of my hands. "I see you managed to finish your popcorn," he said.

"Yeah, I love popcorn." I looked at Linda's pretty brown eyes and smiled.

"See you in school," she said.

" 'Bye Linda. 'Bye Sam," I said.

What Sam didn't know was that he was the captain of the enemy destroyer, and a torpedo with one ugly red smile was cruising his way.

Sam had been in my gym class in seventh grade, and if he had wanted to drop a depth charge on me, all he had to do was tell Linda about what a fool I was the first day of gym.

I had dreaded leaving Lincoln Elementary on Staples' south side and going across town, nearly three-quarters of a mile from home, to

Staples High School. It had grades seven through twelve all in the same building, and a vocational school besides.

Knowing I had to leave Lincoln, where my sixth-grade class ruled, and start all over on the bottom rung caused great distress. At Staples High School I heard you had to have a locker and had to memorize the combination. If you were bad, they sent you to the principal's office.

At Lincoln, there hadn't been a principal's office, although I've since found out that one of the teachers was unofficially the principal. But we didn't know that.

At SHS you had to go to seven classes a day, and you had different books for each class, and teachers expected you to take notes—to literally write down everything they said—and they would hold you accountable for it on the test.

I knew those things because my sisters had been through it. They had told me about it.

"Elementary is a piece of cake compared to high school," they said. One day toward the end of sixth grade, Sam, who was in my class, didn't so much ask our teacher, Mr. Card, as he told him, "Guy isn't going to make it in gym class next year, is he?"

"Oh, he'll do just fine," Mr. Card said.

But the idea was planted in my mind, and I spent most of the summer worrying about taking gym class. From what I had been told, I was going to have special clothes for gym. At Lincoln, we just went outside with whatever clothes we had worn to school, but in seventh grade, you had to change into gym clothes. I realized that, before you could change, you would have to undress.

The thought of undressing in front of Sam and the rest of my male classmates was a frightening prospect. What if Sam or one of his friends told Linda how much fat I really had? I wondered if maybe on the days I had gym, I could put my gym clothes on at home and wear them to school under my other clothes.

Then I learned something even more frightening: At the end of gym, you had to take a shower.

Most of the kids in our neighborhood had homes with showers, but we didn't. I had seen some of their showers, but I had never used one.

Our bathtub was more than just a place to spend Saturday night; it was a place of great adventure, and I would play with toy submarines and other boats of all shapes and sizes. But in seventh grade, after gym class, you didn't enjoy the adventure of a bath; you took a shower, and you had to take it in a big room with all the other kids from your class.

The summer between sixth and seventh grade, I remember lying awake, looking out the window at the mercury vapor street light. I could hear it hum.

It seemed to say: "You have to take gym class. . .You have to take gym class. . .You have to undress. . .You have to take a shower. . .You are fat. . .You are fat. . .You have to take gym class. . ."

It kept saying things over and over in a ghostlike voice.

I wanted to grab the shotgun from my father's police car and shoot out the street light so that it would shut up and let me go to sleep.

Several weeks before school began, we received an official letter from Staples High School. They knew I was to be a member of the seventh grade class, and someone wanted to notify me what I needed to do to prepare to enter SHS. The letter included information about the school lunch program, bus service and what to do if a child became ill.

It also included my class schedule: first hour, math; second hour, social studies; third hour, science; fourth hour, art one day, music the next, and they would take turns getting me every other Friday; fifth hour, study hall; sixth hour, industrial arts one day, gym the next, also taking their turns every other Friday; and seventh hour, English.

I went over the schedule with my mom. I didn't like the looks of it. I had already learned that I was deficient in math, and my artwork had never been singled out to show the class. Social studies and science would be okay, and industrial arts would be a new experience, as would study hall.

I heard that in study hall, if you made one peep, you would have to stay after school for a week. At least that's what my sisters said.

I looked forward to music and hoped maybe someone would notice that I had a nice voice and could sing with lots of volume.

English would be okay, too, if they let me pick out what I wanted to read. But I hoped we wouldn't have SRA boxes like we had at Lincoln, with their different colored levels and their boring stories. I also hoped my English teacher wouldn't care too much about spelling and wouldn't get real excited about diagraming sentences. Diagraming sentences was like getting English mixed up with math.

As we looked at the schedule, Mom noticed that instructions were included concerning what I needed to bring with me for gym. Male students were to report to class with the following: clean, white gym shoes—high tops preferred; white gym socks; red gym shorts (available by special arrangement at Batcher's Department store); and, finally, a supporter. I didn't know what a supporter was, but Mom said we could get that at Batcher's, too, which we did, along with my new high tops and red gym shorts.

The boys' locker room was located in the bowels of Staples High School. Bars covered the lights. This locker room was also used by visiting sports teams, and the bars on the lights protected the bulbs from bouncing basketballs or footballs some visiting player (like a Crosby-Ironton Ranger) might get wild and throw.

The bars, however, made me think of prison, and this locker room was a dungeon; I had been sentenced to it to endure the worst punishment imaginable.

I looked at the bars protecting the lights. I walked over and sat on the concrete bench that was built right out of the wall and ran three-fourths of the way around the locker room.

At the far end of the room, opposite the door I had entered, was a large open area with treelike poles rising from the floor, each with four shower nozzles pointing downward. This was the shower where I would stand with three other guys, who I bet already knew how to take showers.

"All right, listen up!" someone yelled.

I quickly looked at a little, balding man. For a moment I thought I saw a billy club like my dad's in his hands, but closer investigation revealed it was a clipboard. Around his neck he wore a whistle and a stopwatch.

I remembered Sam's prophecy, and now glanced at him as he stood right next to the teacher. Sam had a shower in his house, I knew. *Guy isn't going to make it in gym class, is he?*

The teacher, who I figured was a retired Marine drill sergeant, continued his tirade. I didn't know why he was so angry, but his voice still rings in my ears: "I'm going to issue you a lock. I'm going to give you the combination to your lock. Should you forget the combination to your lock, I'm going to write it across your forehead in Magic Marker. All right, get changed into your gym clothes, on the double!"

Beside me on the concrete bench was my bag with my gym clothes. It was a Heier's grocery bag. Some of the other kids had what appeared to be professional sports bags, with team colors and mascots on the sides.

I reached into the bag from Heier's and took out the high tops, shorts, shirt, socks and the supporter. Although I had been with Mom when we picked these things out at Batcher's, I hadn't actually tried any of them on yet, except for the shoes, to make sure they fit.

My face could have started a piece of paper on fire as I undressed.

I might as well have undressed in the school cafeteria, or at a pepfest in the gymnasium.

I opened the box labeled "Bike" and took out the supporter. I had never seen a supporter before, and wasn't sure how to wear it. I could feel my heart beating at my temples, and I was perspiring so heavily that I wondered if my teacher would consider this an adequate workout so I could be excused from gym for the day.

"Come on! Get dressed! There are laps to run! There are pushups to do! There are more laps to run!" yelled my teacher.

I thought about glancing over at Sam to see how he had put on his supporter, but I was too embarrassed, and I didn't want him to see me looking at him. I thought if I didn't look at anyone, maybe no one would look at me either, and no one would notice that this seventh grader had three stomachs.

I held the supporter. I figured it was like any other article of clothing—the tag should go in the back. I tried to put the great big "Bike" tag in back. It got all twisted up, and I knew I had gone wrong somewhere.

By this time most of the other kids were already dressed and ready to run some laps and do some pushups. I longed for the days of recess and wished Danny could stab this teacher with a frozen drool icicle.

The instructor must have read my mind, because as I was trying to twist the supporter so that the tag would be front, he looked my way and yelled: "Loooook at this, everybody! He doesn't even know how to put on a jock strap!"

I looked up to see Sam laughing at his prophecy come true, and in ultimate humiliation, I sat down on the cement bench, happy I was perspiring so heavily, because my tears looked like perspiration.

I looked over at Steve, who was just about to pull up his red shorts, and saw how the supporter should go. With the eyes of the world on me, and my classmates still laughing, I took off my "Bike" and put the tag in front, where tags aren't supposed to go.

I was the last one out of the locker room, and so the teacher made me run two extra laps. I was the last one back into the locker room, too.

As I took my shower, I knew that I wasn't going to make it. I was sick. I ran and used the toilet that was near the entrance to the shower. It sat right out in the open, and I could feel my classmates staring at me as my head hung over the bowl.

I knew I wasn't going to make it. I was going to have to go home; maybe I could quit school.

The principal's secretary seemed very understanding, and she called my mother. No one was home. There was only an hour left of school, and my mother had planned to pick me up at 3:15, so the secretary gave me a pass to go across the hall and lie down in the nurse's office.

I missed the next two weeks of school. Toward the end of the second week, I wasn't actually sick anymore but was playing up my illness the best I could. I tired of being sick, however, and told Mom that maybe I would feel better if I could go to a movie.

Mom said that if I felt good enough to go to a movie, I must be feeling good enough to go back to school. I quickly checked for a temperature, and I thought my cheeks did feel warm. But Mom took out the thermometer, and it read 98.4.

"You better get to bed early tonight, dear," she said, "because you're going to have lots of make-up work to do when you go back to school tomorrow."

That moment I realized there were things my mom didn't understand, and there was no way to explain them to her. She thought I had a beautiful voice. She loved my chalk drawing of Linda. She always asked if I had any girlfriends. She was always telling Grandma and Grandpa and my aunts and uncles how smart I was, but she never mentioned math.

It would have broken her heart if I had told her that I was ashamed of going to gym with a brown paper bag from Heier's and that I wanted a professional sports bag to carry my gym clothes in.

I didn't know how to tell Mom that she was wrong—that I didn't have a nice voice, I was terrible at art and I was quite dumb. So I just buried my head in her shoulder and cried.

Hope Which Springs Eternal

There is a double standard in the world. What is fine for some-body else may get you in trouble.

Mrs. Stone was one of my teachers at Lincoln Elementary. She had grown up in Staples, a member of one of the town's most prestigious families, had gone off to Teachers Training College and come back to Staples to teach.

I first encountered her in second grade and would later have her as my fourth-grade teacher as well. Mrs. Stone was a very good teacher. She was very nice. She was also short. Quite a few of the kids were just as tall as Mrs. Stone.

My mother had also grown up in Staples, and her family knew Mrs. Stone's family. When families spend their lives growing up together in small towns, they get to know one another.

My mom and Mrs. Stone were friends. Mom asked me daily when I came home from school, "How was Marion today?"

It was quite a revelation to discover that teachers had first names.

I had come to believe that all teachers were either Miss or Mrs. (Until I was in sixth grade the only Mr.'s at Lincoln were Hill and Lindaman, the janitors, and you could call them Roy and Budd.)

Not only did my mother refer to Mrs. Stone as Marion, but most of the time she also called her "cute little Marion." My mother had a way of adding descriptive adjectives before people's names. There was Big Bob, Crazy Karl and a number of other interesting characters, some whose names are best left undisclosed. But Mrs. Stone was the only one I knew to whom Mom had given two adjectives: cute little Marion.

I liked it. It seemed to fit Mrs. Stone.

"Did cute little Marion play the piano in school today?" Mom asked, as I came running in the house to grab an oatmeal revel with raisins she had just taken out of the oven.

Mrs. Stone was quite an accomplished piano player and was the organist at the Methodist church.

"Yeah," I answered, "we learned a new Christmas song. Want to hear it?"

"Sure, honey," Mom answered, as she listened to me sing "Up on the Rooftop." "Did cute little Marion teach you that?"

"Yep. And we get to sing it with the third graders at the Christmas program." As a second grader with a good voice, I could hardly wait.

One day Mom dropped me off at school, and as I was getting out of the car, she said, "Be sure to say hi to cute little Marion."

"Okay, Mom. 'Bye." I ran up to the building, her request firmly planted in my mind.

As I entered Mrs. Stone's classroom, she stood greeting everyone at the door.

"Good morning, Guy, how are you today?"

She really seemed to want to know. This was a nice lady, and I wanted to show her that I really liked her, too.

"Hi, cute little Marion!" I said, as I patted her on her backside.

I had seen my dad pat my mother there a number of times, and it seemed that was something you did if liked someone.

All the kids suddenly stopped what they were doing. The room became immediately silent. Everyone's eyes were on the scene at the door. Mrs. Stone quickly grabbed me and hauled me into the cloak closet.

"Guy!" she exclaimed, her face red.

Two kids who were hanging up their coats ducked out the other end of the closet and shut the door.

"Guy, you mustn't call me that. Why did you do that?"

"Mom calls you 'cute little Marion' all the time, and she told me to tell you hi." So it was my mom's fault.

I think Mrs. Stone realized it was my mother's fault, too, because she seemed to melt. She even smiled and kind of gave me a hug, and then she said, "You mustn't call me that in school, Guy. You must call me 'Mrs. Stone.' Do you understand?"

"Yes," I said, although I didn't really. She hadn't mentioned my patting her, but I figured out on my own that was something she didn't want me to do either.

I came out of the cloak closet looking pretty serious. As I sat down at my desk, Danny looked over at me and asked, "What did she do to you?"

"She's going to talk to my mom," I said.

And Mrs. Stone did.

Mom would tell me sometime later that Mrs. Stone (cute little Marion) couldn't keep from laughing as she told her about the incident.

Mrs. Stone was another molder of dreams in my life, one of those people whose letter I was reading to make some decisions about whether or not I mattered.

Mrs. Stone taught me that I did. Many teachers along the way gave me hope, and I would love to tell you about all of them. The trouble is, so much of what they did was so common, so ordinary, that you would probably find it rather boring. Sometimes all they did was lend a smile or extend a hand or compliment me on the way I was dressed. I wonder if they knew I would carry their smiles with me still today.

I must mention, too, that some of the most important molders of my dreams weren't legitimate teachers in the classroom, but they were teachers nonetheless. I'm thinking of Wilma Kupitz, who was the youth director and choir director at Staples Congregational Church. Wilma taught me to use my gifts for God and not put myself down. And Ray Garland, my Scoutmaster, took off his socks and put them on my freezing feet after my boots broke through the ice on a five-mile hike. Both Mrs. Kupitz and Dr. Garland gave me hope, too.

Three teachers in particular, though, I have to tell you about. They just did their jobs, as millions of others do every day. Maybe they were simply in the right place at the right time. God used them in His usual way—common people in the common circumstances of life.

Mr. Card was my sixth-grade teacher and my first male teacher. When I walked into class that first day, I was surprised to see a man in the room. I wondered if this man was a new janitor, but I guessed not because he had on dress slacks, a white shirt and a tie. I examined him. He looked too young to be a teacher.

By the time I had reached sixth grade, I was quite discouraged about school and life. I had learned I wasn't one of the brightest kids in my class. I was horrible at math. My artwork had been left off the bulletin board. The teacher was always telling me that I had to keep a clean desk, and I just couldn't figure how Mary, who sat next to me, could keep her desk so organized. I sang too loud. No one ever picked me first while choosing teams for kickball. I was never the captain, and I had concluded I would never be the captain or one of the popular kids.

No one deliberately set out to teach me these things, and no one, except a few classmates who made fun of my size, ever purposely meant to hurt me. But I had come to believe I wasn't very good.

I was worried when I realized Mr. Card was going to be my teacher. Men aren't as nice as women, you know. Men are hard and don't have the sympathy women do. At least that's what I thought at the time. And I felt I needed someone who would have sympathy for me; Mr. Card didn't look like he would.

I studied him some more. He walked over to me, held out his hand and said, "Hi, I'm Mr. Card. Norm Card. I'm going to be your teacher."

I had never had a teacher shake my hand before, but I extended my hand and obliged.

"What's your name?" he asked.

"Guy Doud."

"Oh, I've heard about you."

Oh no, I thought. *You've heard that I'm no good at math or art, and that I don't like SRA boxes. You know I sing too loud and have a messy desk. You probably know about my mom and dad and that we're not very rich and we've never been to Disneyland or any place like that . . .*

But I've never found out what Mr. Card knew, and I've never asked him, because he treated me like somebody special. I guess he treated all the kids that way, but what mattered to me was the way he treated me, and it felt good.

Mr. Card was a first-year teacher, right out of college. He did things with us I didn't think teachers were allowed to do. He played with us at recess. He ran around and yelled like a big kid.

We had graduated from kickball to touch football, and Mr. Card was always on one of our teams. He was the quarterback. He didn't let us pick the teams. He divided us up, and he took turns playing for both teams.

One day when he was on my team he said, "Guy, I want you to go out for the pass. Go down the left side. Cut across. When you get to the middle, I'll hit you with the pass."

It gave me such confidence to know that Mr. Card trusted me enough to throw to me. I had come to believe that my role in football was to block, but Mr. Card was giving me my chance to be a receiver.

I lined up as he called the signals. I felt my heart beating in my head. I wanted to catch this ball. I wanted to prove that not just fast, skinny kids could be receivers. I could catch it, too.

The ball was centered. I was off like a slow train, but I was bound and determined to reach my destination.

Mr. Card was elusive in the backfield. Sometimes he would run around back there for what seemed like twenty minutes as we tried to touch him. Just when you thought you had him, he would jump out of the way. This was good as far as I was concerned, because as he was eluding would-be tacklers, I was starting my cut across the center of the playing field.

No one was paying much attention to me. My being a receiver had never been a part of anyone's game plan. It took everyone by surprise when Mr. Card unloaded the football and threw a strike right to me.

He threw it so hard that if one of the skinny kids had been catching the ball, it would have carried him an extra three yards. But it went through my hands, hit my belly, and was starting to bounce away when I pulled it in, smothering it in the folds of my stomach.

I caught it! I was so excited I forgot to run, and Marty quickly touched me. I've since wished we had been playing tackle football because I was so proud after catching that ball that I think I could have carried the entire sixth-grade class into the end zone.

I liked Mr. Card. He came by my desk to check my work, and as he looked it over, he rested his hand on my shoulder. His hand, although extremely heavy and causing me a great deal of anxiety, said, *I like you, Guy. You're okay.*

Sometimes I would raise my hand, kind of hoping that maybe Mr. Card would come by my desk. Maybe his hand would need a place to rest for a moment, and he would use my shoulder.

I worked hard for him, and he told me I was a good worker. I came to believe that maybe doing your best and working hard was even more important than being really smart and getting your artwork up on the bulletin board.

The last week of class Mr. Card handed out awards. It was a full-blown ceremony. He seemed to find something to give everyone. He even gave an award for the person who had to ride the farthest on the bus every day. He got down to the two last awards and said he thought these awards were the two most important of all, for they would go to the hardest working girl and the hardest working boy.

I wondered who would win those awards. I surveyed the room. I figured either Mary or Linda would win for the girls, and I bet probably Sam or Danny would win for the boys.

"The award for the hardest working boy in Mr. Card's sixth grade class goes to Guy Doud."

I heard him say it, but I didn't believe it.

"Guy, come on up and get your award."

I rose from my desk. I was the only one with a steel desk. Mr. Hill had gone to the junior high and brought back a steel desk for me after I had broken my wooden one. I had rocked backwards in it, and one of the legs had broken.

"Hardest Working Boy in Mr. Card's Sixth Grade Class"—that's what the certificate said. Just a plain piece of mimeographed paper;

but it couldn't have meant more to me if it had been a gold statue.

My mom felt the same way, because she left it on the door of the refrigerator, until I took it down about three weeks into seventh grade.

I took it down because I soon learned in seventh grade that maybe working hard didn't matter. Doing your best wasn't good enough.

The person who taught me that so well was my seventh-grade gym teacher. The experience from gym, coupled with the emotional and intellectual adjustment to high school, soon had me feeling worse than I did before I had started sixth grade.

Mr. Card had given me some hope, but I had allowed someone to steal it from me. Halfway through seventh grade hope seemed to have disappeared. I was failing. I hated school. I hated myself.

I felt I deserved to be punished, that I was to blame for being me. People can punish themselves in many ways. Most of us do it rather subtly. I was anything but subtle.

I practiced self-flagellation, striking myself with a wire clothes hanger until I had welts on my thighs. One time I took thumb tacks and pushed them into the welts.

I don't know what I expected to accomplish by punishing myself, but perhaps I felt that if I punished myself, others wouldn't need to punish me.

The rest of seventh grade was a struggle. In sixth grade, kids had crushes on one another, but no one actually seemed to date. Now I was a seventh grader in a building where all the upperclassmen seemed to have girlfriends and boyfriends. Any girl ever wanting to date me seemed about as remote as my being chosen captain of the football team.

But I dreamed of girls—like Linda—and hoped one of them would have sympathy on me, would come up to my locker and say something like "How about a show tonight? There's a good one in town. Why don't we go?"

Gym wasn't the only class that was a struggle. Seventh-grade English was more than I could handle. We had to study Greek mythology and learn the names of all the Greek gods and goddesses. Since it was all made up, I couldn't figure why I needed to know the names of all these gods and goddesses who had never existed. I had a hard enough time memorizing the names of the capitals of African countries, and if I were to spend time memorizing, I would just as soon memorize something important like the statistics of some of the players on the Minnesota Twins.

Not only did our seventh-grade English teacher make us learn the names of the Greek gods and goddesses, but we also had to know their Norwegian names. It was more than I could handle.

Still, I suspected that this teacher, Mrs. Morey, would feel that if I failed, she had failed. And she seemed bound and determined to teach me. She gave me back my hope.

"Could I see you after class, Guy?" she asked.

Oh no, I thought, *what now?*

She had already sent home a notice to my parents that my grades were poor. I figured she just wanted to rub it in.

"Guy, when I called on you to read in class today, you read with a lot of expression and feeling."

That sounded like a compliment, and it made me suspicious.

"Do you like to read?" she asked.

I hated to admit it to her, but I loved to read. I spent hours reading. I just didn't like Greek mythology.

"Yeah," I answered.

"What do you read?"

"Books."

"What kind of books, Guy?"

She was getting very personal.

"Library books."

"From the school library?"

"No, from the city library. Mrs. Albrecht helps me pick them out."

"What are some of the titles?"

Now she was really getting nosey.

I figured that if I told her the titles she might give me credit toward Greek mythology, so I answered: *"The Babe Ruth Story, The Joe DiMaggio Story, The Ted Williams Story, The Jackie Robinson Story, The Warren Spahn Story."*

I hesitated. She was still listening, so I continued: *"The Whitey Ford Story, The Al Kaline Story,* and right now I'm reading *The Harmon Killebrew Story."*

"You like baseball, don't you?" she said, smiling.

I was happy she recognized these people as baseball players, because with girls you couldn't always be sure. Mrs. Morey walked over to her file cabinet and searched momentarily before pulling out a few pieces of construction paper, which she then brought to me.

"This is a poem you might like. Why don't you read it for me?" She handed it to me.

I looked at it. I figured I had to read it. I looked at the title and wondered if this was the same Casey my grandfather always sang about.

I walked to the front of the room and started to read:

It looked extremely rocky for the Mudville nine that day;
The score stood two to four, with but one inning left to play.
So when Cooney died at second, and Burrows did the same,
A pallor wreathed the features of the patrons of the game.

A straggling few got up to go, leaving there the rest,
With that hope which springs eternal within the human
    breast.

*For they thought: "If only Casey could get a whack at
    that,"*
They'd put even money now, with Casey at the bat.

I continued to read the poem. It was interesting. I hoped Casey
would get up to bat. I figured Casey was like Harmon Killebrew, my
favorite Minnesota Twin, and if he could only get up to bat, he would
hit a home run and win the game for Mudville.

The problem was two batters, Flynn and Blake, preceded Casey,
and according to the poem, they weren't very good. Surprisingly, however, both Flynn and Blake got hits, bringing to the plate mighty Casey,
the hero of Mudville.

I knew Casey would come through. He had to. Casey let the first
two pitches pass by for called strikes. The crowd, believing the umpire
to be blind, voiced their disapproval:

*"Fraud!" cried the maddened thousands, and the echo
    answered "Fraud!"*
*But one scornful look from Casey and the audience was
    awed;*
*They saw his face grow stern and cold, they saw his
    muscles strain,*
*And they knew that Casey wouldn't let that ball go by
    again.*

I read with great feeling, looking up from the script to Mrs.
Morey. She sat listening, smiling. Casey had two strikes on him, and
she was smiling! I was nearing the end of the poem:

*The sneer is gone from Casey's lips, his teeth are
    clenched in hate,*

79

He pounds with cruel vengeance his bat upon the plate;
And now the pitcher holds the ball, and now he lets it go,
And now the air is shattered by the force of Casey's blow.

And I knew that Casey, just like Harmon Killebrew, had probably sent the ball screaming over the center field fence. I looked again at Mrs. Morey. Her smile was bigger than ever. I figured she knew that Casey had hit a home run, too.

With "that hope which springs eternal," I read the final verses:

Oh, somewhere in this favored land the sun is shining
*   bright,*
The band is playing somewhere, and somewhere hearts
*   are light;*
And somewhere men are laughing, and somewhere little
*   children shout,*
But there is no joy in Mudville—Mighty Casey has
*   struck out.*

What do you mean, he struck out? Poor Casey. The humiliation he must have felt! The shame. I knew how he felt. It was probably almost as bad as putting your supporter on backwards and being humiliated in front of the whole class. I stood in awe. I looked at Mrs. Morey. She was still smiling.

"You read very well," Mrs. Morey said. "You should be on our school speech team."

I was still thinking about Casey, his striking out, and wondered why the guy who wrote the poem didn't have him hit a home run. Writers could decide how stories ended, and it would have been a much better story if Casey had hit a home run.

"What is the speech team?" I asked.

"We go to meets and compete against other schools. You could do 'Casey at the Bat.' "

There was a team where you could compete by giving speeches? I wondered if there was a contest among the schools to see who could sing the loudest, or who could rock back and forth in their desk the best. I was pretty good at those things, but I wasn't sure about giving speeches.

"You should be on the speech team, Guy."

I got the feeling they needed me. It felt good.

I joined the speech team. Our first contest was in Pine City, Minnesota, several Saturdays later. I had practiced after school with Mrs. Morey almost every night, so by the time the tournament in Pine City came, I had "Casey at the Bat" memorized. More than that, I had become Casey, and whenever I reached the poem's end, my heart bled for the guy. I wished I could tell him that he was a great man, even if he did strike out.

I won a red ribbon at Pine City and eventually went on to represent the Staples speech team at the Minnesota State High School League Tournament.

I learned some time later that a sequel to "Casey at the Bat" existed, called "Casey's Revenge." I was glad to hear it and found a copy of the poem. In this poem Casey once again becomes the mighty home run king and the hero of Mudville. I decided I was glad I knew the poem where Casey struck out, where he felt humiliated. If he had hit a home run in the first poem, I would never have had a chance to get to know him.

At the end of my year in seventh grade, Staples High School held an awards ceremony. Mrs. Morey presented me with an award for my winning participation in competitive speech. I felt the eyes of the entire student body following me as I walked through the gym up the stairs of the stage to receive my certificate.

I thought I heard some students make some rude remarks about my size as I walked past them, but they were unable to spoil this moment for me. Casey may have struck out, but I loved him anyway, and together he and I had succeeded.

As we walked off the stage together, Mrs. Morey told me that over the summer I should try to find a speech to recite the following year. I realized I actually looked forward to eighth grade and to speech.

In eighth grade I would meet Mr. Kopka.

I had struggled through math in seventh grade just as I had struggled through everything, and only my success in speech gave me confidence that maybe I could still succeed in school. Then, in eighth grade, Mr. Leidenfrost renewed my hope for gym teachers, and Mr. Kopka showed me that even math teachers could be okay.

Mr. Kopka had been a Christian missionary to New Guinea, although I didn't know that until quite a while later. I liked Mr. Kopka so much that I also signed up for the German classes he taught.

I discovered in high school that one of the things that made me feel good was being able to help people. I liked being a member of the Safety Patrol, helping little kids cross the street. The librarian needed someone to help check out and catalog books and magazines, and I volunteered. When Mr. Rengel, the athletic director, asked me to manage some of the athletic teams, I felt very important, a fact confirmed when I was given an athletic blazer to wear—just like one of the Cardinal lettermen.

What I enjoyed most, however, was helping Mr. Kopka after school. I did whatever he needed done, and he would give me rides home. Mr. Kopka had so much work to do that he worked at night sometimes, and I would ride by the high school on my bike to see if the light was on in his classroom. If I saw the light, I would knock on the door until one of the custodians answered. I would explain that I had come to help Mr. Kopka.

When I worked with Mr. Kopka, we would talk. I asked him lots of questions; I liked listening to his German accent. One time I was helping him correct some tests, and he had just finished checking my test.

"Look who got an *A*," he said, showing me my paper.

"That's a miracle!" I said, and Mr. Kopka smiled.

"Do you believe in miracles?" I asked.

We had a great discussion about God and miracles, and it was then that I learned he had been a missionary and that he knew Jesus Christ, whom I knew quite a bit about, too. But Mr. Kopka spoke as if he were friends with Jesus in a personal way, and I wished Jesus could be my friend, too.

In Sunday school I had sung "Jesus Loves Me" a million times, and I knew I could pray to Jesus and He would hear me, but I guess what I really wanted was a Jesus who had some skin on, one who could talk back to me, and I wouldn't have to try to figure what He had to say.

I looked forward to helping Mr. Kopka in his room, but what I really enjoyed was his friendship and our talks. Mr. Kopka invited me to attend a gospel concert with him in Moorhead, Minnesota.

In Moorhead, I met Mr. Kopka's fiancée, and we went to the concert together. When they eventually got married, I was an usher at their wedding.

Mr. Kopka never pushed his faith on me. His testimony was the example of his life. I've since learned a poem that aptly applies to Mr. Kopka, my Jesus with skin:

Sermons We See

I'd rather see a sermon than hear one any day;
I'd rather you walk with me than merely tell the way.
The eye's a better pupil and more willing than the ear,
Fine counsel is confusing, but example's always clear.

I wanted to have a close relationship with Jesus like Mr. Kopka did. I wanted to get to know Jesus. But I never suspected I would find Him at the movies.

The Restless Ones, a Billy Graham movie, came to town. I went and got my usual supply of buttered popcorn, pop and Milky Ways and settled down to watch a movie I had heard was about a group of kids who rode motorcycles and had long hair.

This was 1966, and even Staples knew what that meant. It turned out these motorcycle kids weren't so bad, but they needed Jesus, and as I watched the movie, I realized I needed Jesus, too.

I listened to the words of one of the main songs in the movie, and I heard again about a Jesus whom I could know in a very personal way:

'Til by faith I met Him face to face
And I felt the wonder of His grace,
Then I knew that He was more than just a God who
*   didn't care,*
who lived away out there,
And now He walks beside me day by day,
Ever watching o'er me lest I stray,
Helping me to find that narrow way,
He's everything to me.

I had cried at the movies when I saw *Shenandoah,* but the tears I cried for *The Restless Ones* came from somewhere that tears don't come from too often. I was sitting, crying, when Billy Graham came on the screen and spoke directly to me.

"I'm going to ask you to come," he said. "I want you to get up out of your seat and come. Everyone Jesus called, He called publicly. If there are others with you, they'll wait. Come now."

I was alone, so no one needed to wait. I got up out of my seat and went and stood at the front of the theater. Stan Edin, one of the teachers from the school, greeted me and took me to a seat where he counseled me, leading me through a little booklet called "Steps to Peace With God." When we got to the end, I prayed with Mr. Edin to ask Jesus Christ to be my personal Savior.

That night, when I met Jesus, I came to know a Savior who bore my punishment for me. Jesus had known stripes, had been bruised and beaten, and by His stripes I had been healed.

Everything in my life didn't change completely. I was a baby who had not yet learned to walk, but I had found some hope. Many of the feelings of insecurity and worthlessness would take the rest of my life to heal, but I knew I now had a friend who would walk "beside me day by day, ever watching o'er me lest I stray," and this friend became everything to me.

SEVEN

If I Could Be a Teacher

Friendship 7 orbited earth three times in February 1962, and astronaut John Hershel Glenn, Jr. became the first American in space. I remember hearing about it on the radio. I was happy John Glenn had made it into space and had successfully come back. I heard some of the men at church talking, and I knew this was a great thing John Glenn had done. It was good for America.

"We better get on the ball, or the next the thing you know, the Russians are going to be looking down at us from the moon!" said one of my grandfather's friends.

Grandpa just nodded.

I looked out at the moon later that night. It didn't look as far away as I imagined New York to be, and it certainly couldn't be as far away as I knew Russia was.

My teacher had said maybe someday we would land a man on the moon, if the Russians didn't get there first.

I wondered why we had to compete with the Russians, why we

couldn't go to the moon together. But the more I heard about the Russians, the more frightened I became, and the more I understood why we had to get to the moon first.

All around Staples on the government buildings they were putting up yellow and black signs.

"Civil defense signs," Grandpa said.

They put up one of the signs with its funny design on Lincoln Elementary, and our teacher told us it meant that if a nuclear war broke out, Lincoln Elementary had a fallout shelter stocked with water and dehydrated food. We would be able to go into the basement of the school and be safe. We would have to stay in the shelter for about two weeks before it would be safe to come out.

One day we actually went down into the basement and looked at the shelter. I didn't think it looked big enough to fit all us kids in.

If the Russians did drop the bomb while I was at school, I wondered what my mother and father and sisters and baby brother would do. Would they have time to come to Lincoln Elementary and get in the shelter with us?

My teacher said that the Civil Defense Department had a pamphlet that would explain how to build a fallout shelter in your basement at home. We didn't have a basement.

I asked the teacher what those of us who didn't have a basement should do. She explained that just as Lincoln Elementary had a fallout shelter, other government buildings in town had shelters, too. Just look for the black and yellow signs, she explained. She mentioned city hall and the hospital as two places with fallout shelters.

I thought about that for a few moments and realized city hall was the closest to our house. I hoped we would be able to make it there when the Russians dropped the bomb.

The first Wednesday of every month the siren on the fire department sounded for about two minutes straight. It could be heard from one end of Staples to the next. I bet they could even hear it in Motley, seven miles away. The siren usually meant one of three things: it was noon, there was a fire, or it was ten o'clock and the curfew had gone into effect; kids like me better not be out on the city streets.

But when the siren blew the first Wednesday of every month, the teacher told us that it was practice, in case of a nuclear attack or a tornado or other disaster.

"It's the civil defense siren," she said.

Some nights I would hear the ten o'clock siren and check to make sure it was the ten o'clock siren and not the civil defense siren, warning us to retreat to our fallout shelters.

So when John Glenn orbited the earth, I felt a bit better. We were catching up to the Russians. President Kennedy came right out and said that by the time I graduated from Staples High School, America was going to put a man on the moon.

I taped a poster of John Glenn up in my room, right alongside the picture I had of President Kennedy. I liked Kennedy, too, but remembered someone had told my dad that Kennedy was a Catholic.

We had never had a Catholic president, they said. They had told dad that, if Kennedy were elected, he would turn the country over to the pope.

My dad laughed.

I thought about it, though. Some of my best friends were Catholics, and I figured if we had to turn the country over to someone, it would be much better turning it over to the pope than to the Russians.

Not long after Kennedy had been elected, our U-2 spy planes discovered the Russians were constructing missile launch sites in Cuba. President Kennedy ordered Khrushchev to dismantle the sites and to get the Russian missiles out.

I had learned that Kennedy and Khrushchev didn't like each other. Khrushchev had taken off his shoe and had pounded it on the desk at the United Nations as he screamed, "We will bury you." Kennedy had gone to Berlin and told them to take down the wall.

Now the president was not only telling Khrushchev to get the missiles out, but he also sent American warships to blockade Cuba. Suddenly there was renewed interest in Staples in fallout shelters because many felt we were on the brink of nuclear war. When the ten o'clock siren screamed each night that week, I checked to make sure it was ten o'clock.

Khrushchev was stubborn, but Kennedy wasn't about to give in. On October 24 Russian ships loaded with missiles bound for Cuba turned back. On my birthday, October 28, Khrushchev agreed to dismantle the Cuban missile sites and withdraw all Russian missiles from Cuba. It was a good birthday present.

My grandpa said, "Kennedy is a good president."

The pictures of astronaut John Glenn and President John Kennedy still hung on my wall when I started fifth grade in 1963. I remember one day that fall Mrs. Adams, our fifth-grade teacher, left the room momentarily after someone knocked on our door. She quickly came back into the room. She was shaken, and I could tell something terrible had happened. It looked as if she had tears in her eyes. She didn't have to ask us to be quiet and listen; we knew we were going to hear something important.

I thought maybe the Russians had dropped the A-bomb and that the civil defense siren wasn't working.

"President Kennedy has been shot," she said.

My entire class sat in silence. I felt the tears coming but didn't want anyone in class to see me cry.

Why would anyone want to kill such a great man as President Kennedy? I wondered.

I'd seen the movie *P.T. 109* and knew that President Kennedy had barely escaped death when a Japanese destroyer sank his PT boat in the Solomon Islands east of New Guinea. Marooned far behind enemy lines, John Kennedy had led his men back to safety.

I hoped that Kennedy would escape death once again and in a strong voice said: "Maybe he was shot only in the arm and will be okay."

Mrs. Adams smiled gently at me.

School was dismissed for the day.

It was my mother who informed me that President Kennedy had died. I could hold the tears no longer, and my mother also cried as she held me.

I watched it all on television: the president's funeral, the long procession to Arlington National Cemetery, the lighting of the eternal flame. I watched television, too, as Jack Ruby shot Lee Harvey Oswald, and I was confused at what was happening in America.

President Kennedy and John Glenn were two of my heroes. I respected them even more than I did Harmon Killebrew.

One of my friends said, "I'm going to be an astronaut," and he was serious.

I started to wonder what I would be. I had always thought maybe I would just live at home forever. So when I realized that someday I would have to have a house of my own, it caused no small concern on my part.

I didn't think I would enjoy being an astronaut. I was glad men like John Glenn were willing to do what astronauts did, but I had never even been up in an airplane. And ever since I had broken my arm jumping off the Mertens' garage, I was apprehensive about heights. (I had yelled "Superman!" and jumped. It was only about twelve feet up, but I flew right to the ground.)

Some of my friends were talking about going into the army and being soldiers. Some of their brothers were being sent to Vietnam. From what I had heard about Vietnam, it didn't sound like a place I wanted to go. I figured it would be even harder for me to shoot at a person than it would be for me to shoot at a deer.

I thought about being a policeman like my dad, but Staples already had four policemen and was adding a fifth. I knew that whatever I did I would want to live in Staples. My grandpa said the railroad business wasn't what it used to be and that all the glamor had been taken away when the diesel trains replaced the steam locomotives. So I ruled out working for the railroad.

My friend on the corner of the other block was a good Catholic. He sometimes pretended he was a priest and would practice serving me the eucharist. Although he gave me a bit of what he called "the host," he said I couldn't have any of the wine, which was really nothing but some juice anyhow.

One day I gave him my confession, and he told me I had to give him one of my candy bars for penance. He put on robes and wore rings on his fingers, which I had to kiss. He put a cross around his neck and said funny-sounding phrases that he said were Latin, but I wondered if he wasn't really speaking in tongues.

"I'm going to be a priest," he said.

Since I was a Protestant, I decided that I could be a minister, but being a minister didn't sound as exciting as being a priest. I wanted to hear confessions and give out penance.

I decided for a while that I wanted to be a baseball player like Harmon Killebrew, but as I examined the Minnesota Twins, I realized I probably wasn't fast enough to be a third baseman like my hero from Idaho.

Then I thought of Earl Battey, the Twins' "backstop." I figured I, too, could be a catcher. Earl Battey was a great ball player, and he ran slower than I did. I remember once he hit a clean single to right field, but the right fielder threw Earl out before he reached first base. I could do just as well, I reasoned.

My dreams about being a professional athlete died that day in seventh-grade gym, when I realized a guy who put on his jock strap backwards was probably never going to be a major leaguer. I was back to wondering what I could do for a living.

I thought about being president, like Kennedy. But I wasn't sure how you became president. The more I thought about it, I decided I didn't want a job where people wanted to kill you.

My sister Nicki had gone to college to be a teacher. My sister Janice had gone to school to be trained as a beauty operator. I considered those professions, the latter not for long. But as I thought about being a teacher, I started to think about the teachers in my life. Most of them had been women. Then along came Mr. Card. Once I started junior high school, I learned that lots of men were teachers.

Harmon Killebrew, John Glenn, President Kennedy—I had their pictures up in my room, and I cherished my Killebrew baseball card. But suddenly I realized that the real heroes in my life were my teachers: Mr. Card, Mr. Kopka, Mrs. Stone, Mrs. Morey...

The teachers all seemed to have pretty nice cars and houses. I checked them out.

"That's where Mr. So-and-So lives," I would say, pointing out a house to my dad as I rode with him in the police car. I saw a boat and fish house in the yard, and a trailer with the snowmobiles, and I figured if I became a teacher, I would have enough to eat. I would probably even have enough to take some trips and maybe make it to Disneyland.

Nicki told me President Kennedy had arranged it so you could go to college, and the government would give you a loan you wouldn't have to pay back until you taught for a certain number of years.

I thought, "That President Kennedy..." and was happy such a loan was available. I knew my parents couldn't afford to send me to college.

Once Nicki started to teach, I became convinced I wanted to be a teacher, too. She came home some weekends, and all she could talk about were her kids.

I was jealous. I thought maybe she had come to like some of them more than she did me, which, of course, was childish. But her excitement about teaching and her love for her students was contagious, and I caught the bug.

Her first year as a teacher, Nicki was able to buy a brand new car that no one else had ever owned. This was something my parents were never able to do. I knew our minister didn't have a new car, either.

Just a couple of years later, Nicki traded in her shiny red Malibu two-door and bought a new four-door Impala. Some of my friends told me if she wanted a good car she should have bought a Ford, but I stuck up for Chevys because my dad had said they were much better.

The Impala was more car than Nicki needed, but she wanted a car large enough to transport our entire family. She wanted to take us to visit Aunt Renee and Uncle Marvin, and she knew we wouldn't all fit in her Malibu. Aunt Renee and Uncle Marvin lived in Santa Ana, California. Which just happened to be quite close to Knott's Berry Farm . . . and Disneyland.

It was a dream come true—our family on the way to Disneyland in a new car. When I became a teacher, I would have a new car, too, and I would be a teacher like Nicki, who really cared for her students.

Nicki had also become a spiritual mentor in my life, her faith in Christ vibrant and alive. Her example and that of other teachers in Staples comprised the model I would use when someday I would stand in front of my classroom (my new car parked outside within view) and give out penance.

At the end of my junior year in high school, I finally won an election. I had run for Student Council every year and had never been elected. (Mr. Uhrich, the principal, eventually appointed me "member-at-large.") But then I was actually elected to an office: president of the Future Teachers of America Club.

When my term as president began the fall of my senior year, Mrs. Schmidt, the advisor of the FTA, quickly put me to work. Our club was large, with more than sixty members, and we met regularly to discuss the teaching profession. We also helped teachers correct and proctor tests.

Mrs. Schmidt asked me if I would like to help with her seventh-grade math class. I wished Mrs. Schmidt taught a good class, like gym, where I could really make kids work, but I decided seventh-grade math would be an adequate first challenge.

I walked into class and looked at the little seventh-graders. They had a lot to learn about Staples High School. Elementary was a piece of cake compared to high school.

Mrs. Schmidt sat in the back of the room. I was to distribute and proctor a math test. Although I had never had any formal education classes on how to be a teacher, I had been exposed enough to teaching that I understood the proper procedure.

I walked to the blackboard and wrote: "Mr. Doud." I underlined "Doud" several times and pronounced it for them. Mrs. Schmidt seemed pleased.

"I'm going to pass out your test. I will also pass out one piece of scratch paper. If you need more scratch paper or have a question, raise your hand, and I will come to your desk." A good start. I looked at Mrs. Schmidt; her smile told me to continue.

"You must keep your eyes on your own papers. If I catch your eyes wandering, I will immediately rip up your paper, and you will receive a zero on the test. Is that understood?"

I again looked back at Mrs. Schmidt, as my seventh-graders sat frozen. Mrs. Schmidt was really pleased, although she did later tell me that perhaps I had come on just a bit too strong.

95

As I handed out the tests and walked among the seventh-graders, stopping occasionally to rest my hand on a shoulder and answer a question, I thought, *All this and a new car besides. If I could be a teacher. . .well, that would be even better than being an astronaut.*

After graduating from Staples High School in 1971, I did indeed go on to college, where several of my teachers continued to be molders of my dreams and confirmed for me that I wanted to be a teacher.

Of course, when it came time to face my student-teaching stint, I was excited but frightened. What if the kids didn't like me?

As I talked to Jesus about my fear, I realized I should be brave. John Glenn had been brave. But then again, I wanted to be a teacher, not an astronaut.

The Least of These

Dad drove slowly down Main Street as Mom and I searched for the building where I would be rooming.

"It's the Swanke Building, or something like that," I said, checking the address on the paper I held in my hand.

I wiped away the February frost from the side window. The gray Dakota winter sky gave no indication that spring would soon be coming.

I was trying hard to appear calm and in control. My stomach was one big knot, and perspiration ran from my forehead and neck. I had never lived on my own before. Furthermore, tomorrow I was to face a classroom of students as the new student teacher.

I wanted to be a teacher, to try to mold and shape lives in the same way teachers had molded and shaped mine. But now, as we drove down Wahpeton's Main Street, the car's defroster couldn't thaw the chill running down my spine.

"Are you nervous, honey?" Mom asked.

"A little," I lied.

"You're going to do just fine," Mom assured me.

"You've got nothing to worry about, boy," my dad added.

I wondered if my dad had ever experienced fear. I realized he must have, but I never knew it.

We found the building where I was to stay. The apartment was owned by a retired schoolteacher. She was friendly and showed me to my room. It was small, dark and uninviting, but it was also inexpensive.

Dad helped me bring my clothes and things up the long flight of stairs. As we unpacked, Mom surprised me with a box of oatmeal revel cookies.

Once unpacked, my folks decided they had better begin the trip back to Staples. Heavy snow was in the forecast.

"You know how nervous your mother gets when the roads are icy," Dad said.

I walked them to the car. At that moment I realized I was now on my own.

Dad said, "Good luck, kid," as he got behind the wheel.

Mom started to cry as she kissed me good-bye. I hugged Mom for a long time. It felt good to rest my head on her shoulder.

"Jesus is with you, honey," Mom said.

"I know He is, Mom," I answered.

"Come on, woman! We're burnin' gas!" Dad yelled from the car.

Mom smiled, and I shut the door behind her.

I stood on the sidewalk, waving until the car was out of sight. That is a Rice tradition. Grandma and Grandpa always did the same thing. Mom always did it. Aunt Renee, Mom's sister, and my sisters and brother, they all do it, too.

As Mom and Dad drove into the distance, I heard one last honk of the horn, a final note of encouragement. I climbed the long stairs to my room above Main Street.

The following morning, Mrs. Lillian Hackney, my supervising teacher at Central Junior High, welcomed me with enthusiasm. She introduced me to others on the staff and made me feel at ease. Mrs. Hackney obviously loved her job and was good at it. I thanked God that I had been assigned a teacher like her as my mentor.

After only a day of my observing her, she asked, "Well, when do you want to start teaching?"

"Anytime," I said.

"I guess you've been observing teachers all your life; you probably are ready to give it a shot. Why don't you start tomorrow?"

That evening I sat working on my English lessons for the following day. Since my room was poorly lighted and not very appealing, I took my materials and went across the street to Clem's Cafe.

I was finishing my second piece of blueberry pie and ice cream when a group of young kids came into Clem's. I recognized at least one of the kids as a student from Mrs. Hackney's class. I would later learn that his name was Randy.

This group bought some candy from the cashier. I listened to their conversation. Randy's language was peppered with profanity. He and his buddies left the restaurant.

I watched them as they stood outside, surveying Main Street. Randy seemed to be perpetual motion. He bounced up and down and wouldn't stand still. I had noticed him bouncing in his seat earlier in the day.

He lit a cigarette. His friends did, too, and as they all stood smoking in front of Clem's, I wondered if this was Wahpeton's version of a gang. Randy looked as if he would have fit right in with the Jets, one of the gangs from a favorite movie of mine, *West Side Story*.

They walked off down the street, cigarettes hanging from their lips. I thought I heard them clicking their fingers and singing, "When you're a Jet. . ."

I suddenly felt very unprepared to be a teacher.

I called Mom collect and told her that I wasn't sure I would make it as a teacher.

She said, "Don't be stupid," which was exactly the type of direct counseling I needed.

I talked to Jesus that night, too. "I'm not so sure I'm cut out to be a teacher."

"Trust me," He said.

I knelt by the bed in that little room and asked God to use me to teach the Randys of the world, because I figured that if I could reach the Randys, I could probably teach the rest of the kids as well.

"Just love them, as I love you." That's what I sensed Jesus was saying to me: "Love them. As I love you."

It was difficult for me to love some people. I had become pretty good at judging people. Those whom I had judged unworthy were difficult to love. I had quick judgment for some of my male peers who had long hair, and even harsher judgment for those who wore earrings. People who smoked or drank alcohol had one foot in hell, as far as I was concerned. I was able to decide within a few minutes whether a person was a "good Christian," and once I had made up my mind about someone, it was hard to change it.

I had talked to a minister and asked him why he didn't seem more concerned about all the people who were going to hell. I figured that more preachers needed to preach hell-fire and damnation and frighten sinners into repentance. My experience had been that most churches seemed pretty soft on sinners.

I had read "Sinners in the Hands of an Angry God" in Mr. Frisch's American literature class in college and thought more preachers should have Jonathan Edwards' enthusiasm.

The minister looked at me and gently smiled. "Guy, I learned a long time ago that you must hate the sin but never hate the sinner."

I had heard that saying before, but I wasn't sure how you could separate the sin from the sinner.

The minister and I talked about the story of the Prodigal Son. It was one of those parables that was hard for me to understand. I felt the eldest son had gotten a raw deal. It seemed to me that the father should have given the eldest son an even bigger party than he gave the wayward son who had returned home. The younger son didn't really deserve a party at all, as far as I was concerned.

The pastor said to me, "This really isn't the story of the prodigal son; it's the story of a loving father."

That didn't make sense to me. Then something happened that helped me understand God's love for all of us.

Rick was one of the neatest Christians I knew at Concordia College. I was a bit suspect of him, however, because he had a beard. We lived on the same floor of Livedalen Hall.

Once a week, Rick and I would go to a Bible study together. One evening, as I stood waiting for him to finish one of the math problems he was working on, I noticed a poster on the wall above his bed.

It was a pitiful picture: A drunken bum lying in the gutter, an empty whiskey bottle by his side. It looked as though the bum was lying in his own vomit. His trousers were open, and his clothes were filthy. I examined the bum. He personified everything I hated about sin.

The inscription on the poster read: "You love Jesus only as much as the person you love the least." The inscription was followed by a Bible reference: Matthew 25:40. I made a note to look up that verse later.

"Ready to go?" Rick asked, as he grabbed his Bible.

"Yeah," I answered, turning away from the poster.

About a month later, I was sitting in a restaurant in downtown

Fargo, North Dakota. I had felt the need to get away from campus, and I loved the pancakes at a restaurant on Broadway.

Eating seemed temporarily to ease my pain. I had decided I would probably be single all my life. I was getting ready to graduate from college, and I had never had a date. Loneliness consumed me. I prayed and I prayed. I began to wonder whether Jesus really did love me. I had been so faithful to Him, but it seemed as if those I considered downright wicked were prospering, and I was encountering one major obstacle after another.

My mother's cancer had grown worse. Her handwriting in her last letter had been very shaky. Both Grandpa and Grandma Rice had died, and I missed them so.

I had developed rheumatoid arthritis like my grandmother had. It had progressed so far that I needed crutches to walk, and for a short time I was bound to a wheelchair. I wore knee and wrist braces, and sometimes the pain in my joints kept me awake at night. I was undergoing treatment at a hospital in Fargo and had just spent several weeks hospitalized in Moorhead after I had collapsed with pneumonia in both my lungs.

I had been very successful in college and would be graduating *summa cum laude* with a virtually straight-*A* average. I thought of graduating and wondered if I would be able to find a job. Fear gripped me.

My mother couldn't die.

I had been a Christian since junior high, but the love and peace I had felt the night I asked Jesus into my heart seemed eclipsed by my trials and personal struggles. I always seemed to be competing at something, trying to win first place.

I had come to feel that I had to compete for God's love, too—that I had to work to earn His favor. His love came with strings attached, I felt, and soon this legalistic attitude was destroying my joy.

I prayed for a girlfriend, and sometimes as I prayed my prayer became a fantasy. I would imagine myself with a girl, holding hands, embracing. I could see myself kissing her, and as I pictured it, I realized that what had begun as a prayer had turned into lust. I would begin to cry.

I prayed with less and less frequency. How could God go on forgiving? Why bother even asking God for forgiveness when I knew I was going to fail again?

Sin was failure. I couldn't fail. I had to be perfect to earn the reward I so desired. I was punishing myself again as clearly as I had when as a seventh-grader I had struck myself with a clothes hanger.

I had a window seat that day in the restaurant on Broadway. I sat watching the pedestrians as they hurried by. None of them looked very happy. Everyone seemed so serious. *I guess that's the way life is,* I decided.

An old woman came from the north, walking slowly. Behind her came an old man. As they approached the opposite side of my window, I stared at them, my fork suspended between my plate and my mouth.

I had never seen two uglier people. They had to be retarded, I figured, mustering up some sympathy for them. Both had huge cauliflower ears and faces filled with warts and other growths. They were dressed worse than many of the bums who jumped out of boxcars and came begging at our house when I was a child.

I tried not to stare at them. They were both smiling. They were both humming. I heard them humming when they entered the restaurant and sat at the table next to me. Despite their jovial nature, I found them repulsive and suddenly lost my appetite.

The man began to search his coat and finally pulled out a coin purse. "It's my turn to treat," he said.

"You treated last time," said the lady, opening her purse and taking a dollar bill out of her wallet. They didn't sound retarded.

I looked out the window to see two other people heading my way: a mother and her young daughter, holding hands. The girl was like a picture, with her beautiful blond hair and blue eyes, dressed as if it were Easter Sunday. They entered the restaurant.

"Look at the beautiful little girl!" said the old lady with warts.

Her companion had already noticed. "Come here and give me a kiss, sweetie." He leaned over as if he actually expected her to do it.

"I'd like a kiss too," added the lady, also leaning forward in her chair, holding her dollar in her hand.

The girl and her mother stopped and looked at the pair. The mother looked at her princess. The little girl ran to the old man, kissed him on the cheek, turned to the old lady, put both of her soft hands on the rough warty cheeks, kissed her right on the mouth, stepped back and said, "Jesus loves you."

The old lady's eyes filled. "Here, take this dollar, sweetie," she said, as a tear rolled over a wart.

I remembered the poster above Rick's bed: "You love Jesus only as much as the person you love the least."

Now I understood the meaning of the poster.

I realized that Rick, a fellow student, had shown me a Jesus who cared about "the least of these," and a little girl in a cafe in Fargo had changed the way I saw people.

I felt God telling me that if I was going to be a successful teacher, I had to love my students unconditionally.

Later that night, I knelt beside the bed in my small room. Tomorrow students would look to me to be their teacher. Could I help them believe in themselves as my teachers had helped me? Could I show them Jesus' love by loving even "the least of these"? As I concluded my prayer time, I heard Jesus' words: "Love them as I love you."

Soon I was writing my name on the board, telling my students how to pronounce it. I looked into their eyes and saw the same hopes and dreams I had at their age.

I was prepared. Whatever I lacked in experience I made up for in enthusiasm. I looked forward each day to greeting my students. My classes went well, and I felt confident about teaching. Mrs. Hackney provided some good hints and was always there to encourage me, but soon she left me alone with the students, and I came to regard the classroom as "Doud's Domain."

In addition to teaching, I asked Mrs. Hackney if I could direct a play. She was delighted. No one at Central Junior High had directed a play in a number of years, and she encouraged me, although she informed me that I wouldn't have a budget.

I told all my classes about the play. I was going to direct "The Ransom of Red Chief" by O. Henry. I encouraged my students to try out for parts.

I was surprised when Randy walked into my room to try out. I had judged him rather quickly that first night I had seen him with his friends. Now, as he read for a part, I sat smiling. This kid was good. I cast him in one of the lead roles.

Several weeks later I had finished dinner at Clem's Cafe and had driven over to the school for play practice. I entered the auditorium and discovered that something strange was happening in the corner.

About twenty students were huddled there. I had never heard such laughter.

"What's going on?" I shouted, but they couldn't hear me.

"Hey!" I shouted but to no avail.

I quickly walked toward the corner. I pushed my way through the students to discover Randy, who was bent over, his back end pointed toward the ceiling. He was holding a lighter next to the seat of his trousers. Periodically the flame of the lighter would jump, and a little blue jet stream would appear.

"What in the world is going on?" I demanded.

"Randy's lighting—" about a dozen students answered all at the same time.

"Knock it off right now!" I yelled, cutting them off. I had never heard of such a thing and was momentarily unsure of whether to get angry or to take a moment out to watch.

"Randy, come with me!" I demanded, taking him by the arm. We went out into the hall. I couldn't help but remember Mrs. Stone grabbing a second-grader and hauling him into the cloak closet. I tried to disguise my smile, just as Mrs. Stone had.

When Randy and I came back into the auditorium, I heard one of the students ask him, "What did he do to you?"

Randy looked very serious for a moment before he started bobbing up and down in perpetual motion.

What did I do to Randy? You'll have to ask him.

Dr. Ronkin, one of my education teachers at Concordia, had posed many "what if's." "What if a student did this?" "What if a student did that?"

And we would answer. But no one had ever prepared me for someone like Randy, or for someone like the little blond girl in the restaurant on Broadway, who taught me to love each student who comes into my classroom—every person who comes into my life—especially "the least of these."

NINE

Every Adult Needs a Child to Teach—That's the Way Adults Learn

The question was very direct: "Are you a good teacher?"
My mind raced. We are taught humility, but I sensed he didn't
want me to say, "I think so."
With confidence I answered, "I'm one of the best."
"That's what we want," he said and smiled. The question had
come toward the end of the interview.

I had driven to Brainerd, Minnesota, from Wahpeton, North
Dakota, where I was student-teaching. A position at the senior high
school in Brainerd had opened, and I had been called to interview for
the job.

Teaching positions were becoming hard to find throughout much
of the United States as enrollments had substantially fallen. Teachers
nationwide, with years of experience, were finding themselves on
unrequested leaves of absence.

One of my college friends, also majoring in education, said as we
had discussed the job market: "Good jobs are going to be few and far

between. It's going to take a lot of luck."

I drove back to Wahpeton after the interview in Brainerd. I analyzed the questions I had been asked and my answers to them. I hoped I hadn't sounded too proud when I had answered that I was one of the best teachers, but I reasoned, *If I don't think I'm a good teacher, why should anyone else?*

I couldn't think of anywhere I would rather teach than Brainerd. The community had the reputation of a fine school system. The high school was larger than any school I had ever attended, with nearly fifteen hundred students in grades ten through twelve.

The confidence I had displayed during the interview was suddenly shaken. What if I did get the job in Brainerd . . . Would I be able to handle it?

The knock on the door of my classroom in Wahpeton was the secretary informing me that I had a phone call in the principal's office. Mrs. Hackney, my supervising teacher, took over the class as I went to answer the call.

I recognized the voice on the other end. It was Jim Hunt, principal of Brainerd Senior High School. After a few preliminaries, he came right out and told me they wanted to offer me a position.

When I returned to my classroom upstairs, I announced to Mrs. Hackney and my students that I had just been hired in Brainerd.

"Why can't you teach in Wahpeton?" one of my students asked, and I smiled.

A few weeks later, my students hosted a going-away party for me. They wrote poems and served cake and milk.

Randy, for whom God had given me a burden, wrote in his poem:

Mr. Guy Doud
He is quite a teacher!
If he ever needs another job,
He could be a preacher!

I read each of the poems aloud and thanked each of the students who wrote them. I couldn't help but laugh at the girl who wrote the following:

Golly, golly,
Mr. Doud is jolly.
He's not really fat,
He's roly-poly.

And indeed I was. I was now weighing in at almost 330 pounds. I laughed as I looked at my students. Their eyes were still young and impressionable.

I picked up one last poem:

He's going off to Brainerd,
To live there in that town.
He's going to be a teacher,
But he's really just a clown.

At the bottom of the poem the boy wrote, "Just joking, Mr. Doud. You've been a great teacher. Thanks for coming to teach us."

I knew he meant it, and I started to cry.

I always hated it when I started to cry. Men aren't supposed to cry, but I couldn't help it. I had come across a quote in a literature class that had stuck with me: "The world is a comedy to those that think, a tragedy to those that feel."

I realized most people do a little of each, thinking and feeling, but I was predominantly a feeler. And over the years I've come to grips with the reality that that's how God made me. It doesn't take much to set me off. I cried all the way through "Halls of Ivy" when I graduated from Staples High School. I cried when I graduated from

Brainerd Junior College. I cried now, as I said goodbye to the smiling faces of my students from Wahpeton.

I almost cried when I first saw my room at Brainerd Senior High School. The school itself is a beautiful facility, but I was on the bottom rung of the seniority ladder, so I was given room A-110, which was small and windowless.

I spent the few days before school began preparing lesson plans and handouts, organizing books and audiovisual materials. I felt I could never be adequately prepared.

I wondered what I could do to decorate my room, whose walls and bulletin boards were bare, white and uninviting.

I marveled at Mr. Nowatzki's room across the hall. A veteran teacher, Mr. Nowatzki was prepared. A student entering his room would encounter the Starship *Enterprise* on its mission to "seek out brave new worlds and to boldly go where no man has gone before." Mr. Nowatzki taught science fiction, and the *Enterprise,* suspended by fishing line from his ceiling, was only one of the models and posters he had in his room to stimulate student interest.

I looked at my room. It was a "brave new world" where I would teach speech, basic English, composition, short story and film. What could I do to decorate it? Flying question marks and exclamation points? Authors' faces peering down at the students from the ceiling? Posters of Chaplin, Keaton and Hitchcock?

As I stood contemplating a decorating plan, one of the janitors poked his head into my room. "You must be one of the new teachers," he said. "Working late already," he added.

I looked at the clock. 5:30 p.m. We introduced ourselves.

"You've got the hot box," he said.

"I suppose it will get stuffy in here when it's full of students," I commented and then added, "Sure wish the room had a window."

"You could bust a hole in that wall," the custodian joked and pointed to the north wall that bordered the hallway.

Although a hallway was on the other side of the wall, a window there wouldn't be such a bad idea, I thought, realizing it wasn't practical.

"Yeah, thanks," I responded.

"Well, good luck," he said and was off down the hall.

I knew I couldn't "bust a hole" in the wall, but could I make a window there? I went to the English Resource Center down the hall and found a roll of green cardboard used for covering bulletin boards. I made a square of it about five feet wide by five feet long. I took it back to my room and taped it to the northern wall. I cut out some letters to attach to it. The letters read: "Pretend this is a window."

There, I thought, *it isn't much, but I have my window.*

One morning a few weeks later I came into my classroom. I glanced toward my imaginary window. It had been transformed! Someone had cut out real curtains and hung them on the sides of the green cardboard. Paper bouquets of flowers were blooming "outside." Paper birds flew through the green sky. I liked this sabotage, but who, I wondered, had sewn curtains and planted flowers?

Later that day, Mrs. Paulson, one of the cleaning matrons in charge of my part of the building, asked me how I liked my curtains and flowers.

I remember vividly so many other things that happened that first year of teaching in 1975. I was twenty-one. I weighed 327 pounds. I made $7,500 a year and thought it a fortune. I was idealistic, excited and ready to be the teacher.

Just as I did when I first took over Mrs. Schmidt's class as a senior in high school and president of the Future Teachers of America Club, I wrote "Mr. Doud" on the board the first day of school and explained to the students how to pronounce my name.

Doud is really quite a simple name. Most who have it spell it

Dowd. I heard once that we used to be O'Dowds. I don't know why we dropped the *o* or why we changed the *w* to a *u*. It was one of the questions I never got around to asking my dad.

The one time I did ask my dad something about our family tree, he told me that we were related to Mamie Doud, who married President Eisenhower. But we never got cards from them at Christmas or anything like that.

Whenever I write "Doud" on the board and explain how to pronounce it—something I must always do or I end up being *dude, dub, doube, dud,* or some such variation—I wish I knew more about my family tree. I have it on my list of things to do someday.

I've received marvelous offers in the mail, informing me that for $59.95 I can obtain a copy of the Doud genealogy. For that price they will also send me a copy of our coat of arms. Who knows, I may descend from royalty and be in succession to the crown.

I'd like to know this, because as I write "Doud" on the board, I could tell my students, "Listen to me, I descend from royal stock, you know."

Maybe if students knew I was royalty, they would be more interested in split infinitives and dangling modifiers.

I was shocked as I began to teach that some of my students could have cared less about what I wanted to teach them. I admit split infinitives aren't the most interesting thing to study, but I thought my students should know that, in the opinion of most usage experts, it's better to split an infinitive than to displace an adverb.

It's difficult to get interested in split infinitives and displaced modifiers when you're struggling to survive. As I read the journals I assigned my students to keep, I saw how broken homes, alcoholic parents, abuse, neglect, and the absence of Christian faith and values in many homes were breeding destruction.

My first quarter at Brainerd High School, I was assigned to teach a contemporary short-story class. A girl I'll call Kelly sat three seats from the front. Kelly was a small girl without a smile. Her blond hair didn't quite make it to her shoulders. Her eyes always seemed to be directed at her desk, and she never talked unless asked a question. A junior, she was not doing well in my class: incomplete assignments, failed tests, no class participation. I was frustrated at my inability to motivate her and other students like her.

Near mid-term, I sent a letter to her parents, informing them of their daughter's imminent failure, hoping they would encourage and help her. I tried speaking kindly to her. I offered extra help. She didn't respond, and her performance didn't change. She was going to flunk.

I collected the journals on Friday. They would be my weekend reading. I had given a journal assignment the day before.

"Evaluate the class to this point," I had suggested. "Or write a narrative of your own, or write something about yourself that you think I would be interested in knowing."

I attended the football game that evening, then went home to my apartment, a two-room efficiency I rented from a retired social-studies teacher. I had discovered my beginning teacher's salary wasn't the fortune I thought it was.

I fixed myself a triple serving of butter brickle ice cream and sat down to read journals. Kelly's was the first I read.

> *Mr. Doud, I know you don't like me because I'm*
> *dumb. I'm not doing good in your class. I just want*
> *you to know I'm not as dumb as you think I am. You*
> *see, last summer I had an abortion....*

She went on to explain how she had wanted to get married and have the baby. Her parents would not permit it. She had run away from home. She was returned. She was forbidden to see or speak to her boyfriend. Then her boyfriend's family moved out of town.

She apologized for not being interested in my class. "I've been thinking about killing myself," she wrote. "I don't want to live if I can't be with my boyfriend."

She ended her journal entry by stating that she had written what she did because she thought I was a "nice man who always smiled at her" and "maybe I cared."

I wrote a long response in her journal. I told her that I did care and apologized for not being more sensitive to what was going on in her life. I told her not to give up. The feeler inside of me cried as I realized she had been carrying all this pain inside of her, and I had been unaware of it.

Monday came. I planned to return the corrected journals to Kelly's class when it met after lunch. I was somewhat apprehensive about seeing Kelly and hoped what I had written in her journal would open up some dialogue between us.

After first hour ended, I dashed into the English Resource Center for a few sips of coffee. When I came back to my class to start second hour, I found two short-story books on my desk. A note was sticking out of *Twenty-Five Short-Story Masterpieces.*

The note read, "Mr. Doud, here are my books. I'm dropping out of school. Kelly."

In my short teaching career, I had never known anyone to drop out of school. I never remembered anyone dropping out of Staples High School. I wondered what students did who dropped out and in particular what would happen to Kelly.

When fifth hour came, I asked the other students if they knew why Kelly had dropped out of school. One girl thought Kelly was working full-time and was going to go to an alternative school, but most of the students didn't seem even to know whom I was talking about.

I passed back the journals, but I held on to Kelly's in hopes she

Grandpa Guy takes a stand in front of his "office."

Guy's dad, Jess Doud, always wore his hat tilted to one side, in his own cocky way. ▶

Guy hugs a pal and stares down the camera.

▼

▲
Jess, baby brother
Pat, and Guy all prac-
tice saying ''cheese.''

◀ Jess and Jeannette,
Guy's parents, both
brought painful
pasts to their
relationship.

Grandparents Mayme and
Guy Rice provided Guy with
''a first-class dinner and a
generous allowance'' for
helping with the flower and
vegetable gardens.

Boy Scout Guy at thirteen ▶
years old shows the results of
all those oatmeal revel
cookies around his middle.

 College student Guy, weighing in at more than three hundred pounds, appears in Shakespeare's ''Twelfth Night'' as Sir Toby Belch.

Guy plays the man of La Mancha (left) at the Brainerd Community College Theatre.

▼

▲
Tammy and Guy appear
on their wedding day
with Guy's dad and his
soon-to- be wife, Ruth
(Tammy's mother).

Guy's family pauses ▶
for a moment during
a recent Minnesota
outing. (From left)
Seth, Luke, Jessica,
Zachary, and Tammy.

◄ Kent Soderman poses in his graduation gear.

Guy jokes with the president while holding the Crystal Apple and the poem "Molder of Dreams." Tammy listens in.

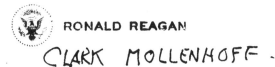

RONALD REAGAN

CLARK MOLLENHOFF.

You are the moulders of their dreams - the Gods who build or crush their young beliefs of Rt. or Wrong.

You are the sparks that sets aflame the poets HAND or lights the flame of some great singers song.

You are the God of the young, the very young.

You are the guardians of a mil. dreams. Your every smile or frown can heal or pierce a heart. Yours are a 100 lives, a 1000 lives. Yours the pride of loving them, the sorrow too. Your patient work, your touch make you the God of hope that fills their souls with dreams — to make those dreams come true.

President Reagan's handwritten version of "Molder of Dreams" as it appears on the presidential note card.

might stop by my class. I wanted her to read what I had written, to know I did care. She was more important than the short stories we had been reading; I wanted her to know that. But I never saw her again.

I felt like a failure. For six weeks she had sat three feet from me, but I had been more interested in Faulkner and Hemingway than in her. Some things were even more basic than reading and writing and arithmetic, but I wondered how I could teach that to my students.

Then I realized that is what they were teaching me.

In a discussion class I was teaching the following year, we wrote on the board a list of problems youth face in society. Students had identified areas such as getting along with parents, making a career decision, doing well in school, peer pressure, changing sexual values, drugs, feelings of alienation and loneliness, suicide, alcohol, physical and sexual abuse, and a number of other challenges they were facing.

"Pick one of the topics we've listed," I instructed, "and write about how it has had an impact on your life. Please don't identify yourselves, because I'm going to read some of your papers to the rest of the class."

The following day I collected their papers and began to share some of them with the class.

One boy wrote, "I wish I could talk to my parents. I sit in my room and get high and listen to my music. My parents don't know I smoke."

A girl explained her situation this way: "I feel like I have to have sex with the guys I go out with or they will drop me, and then after we have sex they drop me anyhow."

I read of another girl's dilemma: "I feel intense pressure from my parents to get straight A's. If I don't get A's, I'm no good. Sometimes I wish I was just average."

What shocked me most, however, as I read their papers, was that so many of them wrote about being lonely. I thought peer pressure and drugs and alcohol were the most significant problems, but the student who wrote, "I feel so all alone, like there is no one I can talk to," voiced the sentiments of a majority of students in my class.

So I studied their faces when I was on hall duty. Hall duty is something I was never trained to do. I've never been evaluated on hall duty and am still not sure whether I do it correctly. I tried to be clearly visible and greeted any student who looked my way.

When I was on hall duty, I overheard many conversations. I learned a lot about my students as I listened in.

With only a minute before class began, I encouraged those students still talking by their lockers to hurry to class. I walked down the hall to stand by the door to my room. I greeted my students as they came down the hall.

"Hi, Bill. How are you today?"

"Just great, Mr. Doud," he answered.

Most of the kids were respectful. Some of them were clearly smarter than I, and it frightened me. I stared into their eyes. I didn't have to look far to see hope alive in most of them, but some were distant and nondescript. Some invited engagement. Some asked to be left alone. I tried to read the eyes, to understand.

Three guys approached me together. I wasn't very fond of black leather and studs. "What are you going to do this weekend?" I asked, as they entered my room.

"Party hearty!" they answered in unison.

Calvin was a farm boy. He understood the work ethic. He was a very bright young man, but what I had to teach didn't interest him all that much. His papers were about hunting and fishing and four-wheeling, and I wished I could relate better. He entered the class.

These two were cheerleaders. They wore their uniforms. One carried a hairbrush in her hand. She always had a hairbrush. She would sit down, open her purse, take out her mirror and check her makeup—which she had checked only moments ago in the girls' lavatory. They giggled their way to their seats.

This one beat me to the punch, "Hi, Mr. Doud! You're looking good today. You going to watch the Vikings this weekend?" And a dozen other questions. I appreciated his enthusiasm.

Here came Shon. When I arrived at school at 7:30 this morning, he was sitting on the stairway nearest my room. I greeted him then, and he had looked my way and turned red before he nodded his head.

I greeted him again: "Hi, Shon, how are you?"

"Fine." That's what we're expected to say.

"What are you going to do this weekend, Shon?"

A moment's hesitation before he looked me in the eyes. "I'm going to see my mom."

Is she hospitalized? I wondered. Or maybe his parents, like so many parents, were divorced.

"Don't you get to see your mom very often?" I didn't want to intrude, but I wanted to know.

As if he had been waiting six weeks to tell me this, with new energy in his voice, he said, "I haven't seen her in nine years. She deserted us."

He waited a moment before walking by me into the room.

"I hope it goes well for you, Shon." But I wasn't sure he heard me.

Soon the room was filled with thirty souls. The bell rang. I was the teacher; their eyes were on me.

The following hour I continued to read the papers written by my discussion students. A girl wrote, "Making a career decision is what I think most about. I have to find a job that is satisfying and pays well. I think I'd like to be a flight attendant and see the world."

I asked the class, "How many of you have ever thought of becoming a teacher?"

No one raised a hand.

"There's a need for good teachers," I lobbied, as I grabbed the next student's paper.

> *My family has been plagued with problems relating to drinking. My brothers usually drank a lot when they were in high school. Their grades were not very good, and they all dropped out.*
>
> *One day while I was at work, I had some visitors. They told me that I had to leave work right away because of a family emergency. I didn't ask no questions, I just changed my clothes and left.On the way to the car one of them spoke up and told me that something had happened to my brother.*
>
> *"Is he all right?" I asked.*
>
> *He just shook his head and said, "No, your brother has been killed in a car accident."*

I continued to read this student's paper:

> *If the fact that my brother's death isn't enough on my mom, I might mention that my dad drinks very heavily. After my brother's funeral my dad decided to get a divorce. My mother started to drink. I'm watching her decay before my eyes. I told her that she's got to stop, and that if she continues, she's going to kill herself.*

I looked up at my students. They sat quietly, listening. *Whose story was this?* I couldn't tell by looking at them. I continued:

> *Two weeks after my brother's funeral, we got the autopsy back from the examiner. We found out that my brother was drunk at the time of his accident. It was*

118

a head-on collision, and the steering wheel pushed through his chest and tore the big artery from his heart by the roots.

I finished this line, but I couldn't swallow the tears anymore. My class sat silently out of respect. They understood, too.

I read the last paragraph:

It's too bad that something like this has to happen to make people realize what they're doing to themselves and others. Maybe if people would take a hold of something solid—like faith in Jesus Christ—maybe then and only then will the troubles of our time be solved.

I stared at my class. A few of them were also crying.

I reread the last line, "Maybe if people would take a hold of something solid—like faith in Jesus Christ—maybe then and only then will the troubles of our time be solved."

"Those are his words, not mine," I said.

Those first weeks of teaching, I discovered I would learn as much from my students as they would from me. The words of one of my college education professors came back to me: "Every adult needs a child to teach; that's the way adults learn."

Pseudolous the Slave Finds Freedom—and Gymnasia

Taco Towne was my favorite eating establishment in the Brainerd area. After finishing a long day at school, I wasn't anxious to go home and cook for myself, so most nights I would drive out to Taco Towne, which was only a home run north of the Paul Bunyan Amusement Center.

As I drove by Paul Bunyan (the world's largest animated talking man), I would glance toward him, and he seemed to say, "I'd like to join you for some tacos, Guy, but I have to work."

But I never had tacos at Taco Towne. I loved their spaghetti, and I loved their chicken, and I thought their pizza was about the best.

I could seldom decide which of my favorites to order, so I would usually have a full order of spaghetti, half of a chicken and a small pepperoni pizza. It was a lot to eat, but I was hungry after a long day involving students in intellectual exercise.

However, I could seldom finish all I had ordered. So I would take a piece or two of the chicken home for a midnight snack, which I would have along with my usual evening three-scoop bowl of butter brickle ice cream.

I really would have preferred going home each evening and having dinner with my family, but I didn't have a family at home. So the folks at Taco Towne, whether they knew it or not, were my family.

The lady who ran Taco Towne was always nice to me and called me by name. I think she appreciated my business. I looked forward to her greeting each night as I entered Taco Towne.

Eating there also saved me time, because soon I didn't have to say much of anything; the waitresses could read my mind.

"You going to have the chicken, spaghetti and pizza tonight?"

They didn't even bother giving me a menu.

Toward the end of my meal, they would say, "You want a doggie bag to take that extra chicken home in."

It wasn't a question; it was a statement. If I had gone to another restaurant, I would have had to explain all these things that the waitresses at Taco Towne somehow seemed to know.

I also ate at Taco Towne because I didn't have any homeowner's insurance on my trailer. After my mother died, I couldn't find anyone who knew how to make pot roast like she did, so I tried to make it myself.

I put it in the oven before I went to Sunday school, just like Mom always did. I had peeled about a half-dozen potatoes and a bag of carrots and hoped that would be enough. I tried to remember how Mom did it. I knew I had to add flour to the water to make the gravy.

I was running late this particular morning. Not only did I have to teach Sunday school, but I also had to preach. So I quickly made sure that I had enough water around the roast, potatoes and carrots. Then I dumped in two or three cups of flour and stirred it into the water, hoping that my gravy would be as good as my mother's and grandmother's. It looked a bit thick, but I figured I could add a little

Kitchen Bouquet when I got home from church.

The battery in my smoke detector was dead, so the detector remained silent despite an ocean of smoke that greeted me when I returned home from church. It got even worse when I opened the oven door. I hoped this didn't mean my roast was ruined.

I quickly took it from the oven, set it on one of the burners, removed the lid from the pot, and beheld something that looked like a smoking volcano. The flour mixed with the water had not made gravy. A truckload of Kitchen Bouquet could not thin the crusted, burnt, bread-like matter that had grown around and over the roast. The potatoes looked like hunks of lava, and the carrots had disappeared, most likely consumed by the substance surrounding the roast.

I was disappointed. I had been anticipating this meal since I had said amen at the end of my sermon. I stared into the roaster. Sympathy could not salvage this meal. I used my tongs to remove it from the pan. I felt like crying as I tossed it into the garbage. I took the garbage out to the trash can, said good-bye to my roast beef, jumped into my car and went to Taco Towne.

They didn't have roast beef at Taco Towne, so I had the spaghetti, chicken and pizza.

I don't think I've ever let Taco Towne know how much I appreciated it. Places play a part in shaping lives, too, and Taco Towne was always there for me.

One standard evening, I had gone to Taco Towne to eat, had finished my usual meal and was on my way out the door. I was thinking about school in the morning. Teacher workshops were beginning for a new school year. I had finished my first year, enthusiasm undaunted, and was looking forward to another year.

I had just reached the exit of Taco Towne when Julie got to the entrance. She was with her boyfriend. I smiled at them.

Julie had been one of my students the previous year. She had helped "break me in." I didn't recognize her boyfriend, but Julie said to him, "That's Mr. Doud. I had him for English."

I don't know why, but she kind of whispered it to him. And then she saw me looking at her and knew that I had seen her tell her boyfriend she knew me. She knew that I knew that she knew that she had told him, so she looked at me and said, "Hi, Mr. Doud."

"Hi, Julie." Always happy when I can remember former students' names.

An awkward moment followed our exchange of greetings. I was unable to exit, and they were unable to enter through the same door, so I took the initiative and stepped aside.

Julie is a typical person, so she felt that she needed to say more than just hi. She looked at me and asked, "Are you still teaching, Mr. Doud?"

I was proud to answer, "Yes, Julie, I'm just getting ready to start my second year."

I wondered how old Julie thought I was. I had discovered that students were very poor when it came to guessing teachers' ages.

"Are you married yet, Mr. Doud?" she asked.

My marital status was a topic of interest among some of my students. One student suggested the names of several female teachers in our building, whom, he said, I should "go after."

I didn't tell him or the others who attempted to be matchmakers that I had never dated anyone and was so self-conscious about my weight that I had decided no girl would ever accept my invitation to do anything. I had concluded I was to be single, and that was all right, because Jesus had been single, too.

"No, Julie, I'm not married."

I didn't try to sound sorry for myself, but that's the way I sounded. I sounded very alone.

Julie was sensitive. She detected the self-pity in my voice, and she wanted to say something to cheer me up.

"You'd be kinda cute if you lost a hundred pounds." She meant it in a nice way.

"Well, thanks, Julie. I hope I can lose a hundred!"

She and her boyfriend entered Taco Towne through the door I had exited and stood holding open.

"Have the spaghetti and the chicken," I said. "It's delicious."

"We love the pizza," Julie said.

My chicken and I went to my trailer and had a five-scoop bowl of butter brickle ice cream. I could hear Julie's words. I would be "kinda cute" if I lost a hundred pounds.

I had tried to lose weight. I would starve myself for a week, then weigh myself to find that I hadn't lost but rather gained.

I kept thinking about what Julie had said.

I cried to God, "Lord, You say that You are no respecter of persons. Why is it that some people can eat and eat and never gain an ounce, and I look at a Milky Way and gain ten pounds?"

It wasn't fair. I thought about the going-away poem one of the students had written:

> *Golly, Golly*
> *Mr. Doud is jolly.*
> *He's not really fat.*
> *He's roly-poly.*

Everyone did think I was jolly. I had a marvelous sense of humor, people commented. The humor, however, was a mask that hid my loneliness and pain.

I dreamt of sharing my life with someone. I wanted a partner who would be there to help bear my sorrows and share my joys.

It would also be nice, Lord, if she knew how to cook and could make roast beef like my mom's, I thought.

I would see children at play and think of having a child of my own—bedtime prayers and story times, and some little one trusting me and needing me for the basics of life. I burned, not simply for physical touch, but for spiritual and emotional union.

I knew no one could love me more than Jesus, who loved me despite my size. If I lost a hundred pounds and became "kinda cute," Jesus would not love me any more than He already did.

I knew that, but my severe obesity had become a stumbling block in my relationship with Christ. My food consumption at times had become gluttonous, and my weight was harming my body, a temple for Christ's Holy Spirit. I had to lose weight like an alcoholic has to quit drinking. I was addicted to food, and it was destroying me physically, emotionally and spiritually. It was also the major factor keeping me from reaching out for female companionship.

"One day at a time, sweet Jesus, that's all I'm asking from you." The song had been one of my mother's favorites. In her years of sobriety, she said she always had to take it "a day at a time."

"If I can't make it through a whole day," she said, "I break it down into hours and then minutes. And I ask myself, 'Can I make it through this minute without a drink?' And I know that with God's help, I can. I can do all things with Christ's help."

Could I overcome my addiction a day or an hour or a minute at a time, trusting Christ? The answer to that question would decide my future.

I had tried some of the world's ways to fill my loneliness. I had begun experimenting with alcohol, something I had never touched during high school or college; I had become busy and involved and was proud that people called me a workaholic and a perfectionist.

Alcohol only made matters worse and left me feeling guilty. I would eat more and work harder, so desiring the approval of others.

As I faced the question of whether or not I could trust Christ to help me one day at a time, I realized that trusting Him required obedience, and obedience was the pathway to joy. "Trust and Obey," a song I had sung recently in church, suggests, "There's no other way to be happy in Jesus, but to trust and obey."

I would "trust and obey."

It was a daily struggle. I starved myself. Gone from my diet were sweets, breads, french fries, fatty meats, butter, pizzas—all the foods I loved. I got so sick of tomato soup that I didn't care if I ever tasted it again. I would go to bed hungry, wake up hungry, go through the day hungry.

By the beginning of my third year of teaching at Brainerd High School, I had lost more than 125 pounds. I had become obsessed with losing weight.

But somewhere in the process, I had taken my eyes off Jesus and put them on myself. My goal became to lose weight rather than to obey Christ. Strangers praised me and told me how nice I looked and what a marvelous job I was doing. No one had ever complimented me before on my appearance, except family. Consequently, I became as addicted to losing weight as I had been to food, and I made bad choices regarding my diet.

Then I read a story in the Minneapolis *Star Tribune* about a seventeen-year-old girl from a small school in rural Minnesota. A straight-*A* student, this beautiful young girl was also captain of her cheerleading team.

The article reported that the girl's boyfriend had told her that her "butt was too big." Humiliated, and feeling she was obese, the girl began to take laxatives regularly and force herself to regurgitate. She starved herself down to eighty-one pounds before she was confronted.

Treatment was deemed necessary, so she was placed in a center in the Twin Cities. She remained there only a short time, as she refused to comply with the treatment.

After being sent home from the treatment center, this girl continued to force herself to regurgitate. Any food she ate caused guilt and fear.

One day she drove the family car out to a park near her hometown. She took two gallons of gasoline from the car's trunk, poured it over herself and set herself on fire.

The note she left behind explained that she just couldn't stand living with herself.

I read the story and wept profusely. I understood how the girl felt. I had become almost as obsessed with losing weight as she had been. I, too, would often force myself to vomit. I weighed myself as soon as I got out of bed each morning. If I had gained a pound, my day was ruined. People would stop praising me, I felt, if I regained weight, and I needed their praise. I was addicted to others' approval.

Why hadn't the girl reached out for help? Why couldn't I? To whom do you go for help?

That's a particularly difficult question if you are one whom everyone else looks to for help. I had always given the impression I had it all together, had my spiritual life in order. I had counseled hundreds of people, saved marriages and kept others from suicide. But to admit that I, too, was struggling would be to admit I wasn't perfect.

The battle continued inside me for more than a year. Then, as I was finishing my third year of teaching, an opportunity arose to attend a summer workshop at the Johnson Institute in Plymouth, Minnesota. My school district wished to send various teachers and administrators to the Institute to be taught about chemical dependency. Those sent would then return to lead workshops and train others.

I volunteered to attend. I had heard much about the Johnson Institute. Begun by Reverend Vern Johnson, the Institute had trained thousands of people to understand how alcoholism affects an entire family.

The first two weeks of the Institute involved training. As I listened to the lectures concerning roles played in the family, I identified myself as both a "family hero" and "a lost child."

The "family hero" often feels it his or her responsibility to fix the family, to be a savior and make sure that the family reputation is safely guarded. When my sisters moved away and I became the oldest child at home, I somehow felt it my responsibility to protect my mother, father and younger brother, as if their salvation were in my hands. If you feel that way, you can begin to notice the nail holes in your hands.

A "lost child" never seems to cause any real problems but is often absorbed with him or herself. I thought of the hours I spent alone reading.

As I listened to the lectures, I couldn't believe that the people at the Institute knew so much about me. Toward the end of the three-week training session, one of the lectures concerned feelings and how to get in touch with them and express them. We talked of the need for trust, compassion and understanding; we talked, too, of the need for honesty and confession. This lecture was a prelude to the two days we would spend in small groups, sharing with one other.

I sat through those two days with eleven other professional people. We were told that whatever we shared would go no farther than that room. We created an atmosphere of trust, and after the first person spilled the contents of his heart and soul, the rest followed.

I was a good listener. I was a good encourager. I couldn't believe that people were carrying around such heavy baggage.

We reached the end of the two days, and everyone had shared— except me.

One of the counselors looked at me. "Guy, do you have anything you would like to share?"

"I hope everything works out for everyone, " I said, tempted to add, "I'll be praying for all of you." But I didn't.

"Guy, I think you're miserable inside." The counselor spoke with a great deal of compassion.

One by one, others in the group shared things they had observed during our three weeks together. There was no judgment; they just held up a mirror to my face.

"You think you are self-sufficient, and you don't need anybody," one person said. Then he added, "I get the feeling you think you're better than I."

The truth was, I didn't feel worthy of their friendship.

The lady sitting next to me put her hand on my shoulder and, with all the compassion a voice can carry, said, "Go ahead and tell us about Guy."

For about the next two hours I shared things I never thought I could share, and when it was over, I felt clean inside. Secret sins were secret no more. Jesus had been present in that small room. My confession in front of people confirmed for me that Jesus had heard me and had forgiven me.

I left the Johnson Institute wishing people knew that churches were places where they could bring all their sin, their entire load, and dump it at the foot of the cross. I wondered how successful churches had been at letting people know that. Christ Jesus died because I'm not perfect, and it's acceptable to admit that. If people knew doubts were normal and others wouldn't judge them for doubting, maybe they would feel the freedom to be honest.

I went to the Johnson Institute with what I had thought was a mighty faith in Christ. I left with faith the size of a mustard seed but learned that with it, Jesus and I could move mountains.

Later that summer I was cast in the lead role in a community production of "A Funny Thing Happened on the Way to the Forum." I played the role of Pseudolous, a slave who is promised his freedom if he faithfully carries out service to his master. At the end of play, Pseudolous is granted his freedom and, as a bonus, is told that he can choose one of the local courtesans for his wife. Pseudolous chooses Gymnasia. Every night at the end of the play, Gymnasia and I would run off together into the proverbial sunset.

The girl who played Gymnasia made me very uncomfortable, because I thought she was the most beautiful girl I had ever seen. Unfortunately, her costume in the play consisted of black leather and studs, and she carried a whip. Despite the costume, I could not help but notice the gentleness of her brown eyes and the sweetness in her soul, nor did her striking figure go without notice.

The last week of the show, Gymnasia asked me: "What are you going to be doing the rest of the summer?"

"Oh, probably getting ready for school to start," I answered.

"It would be fun if we could get together once in a while," she said.

"Yeah..." I was nervous now. "That would be great . . . why don't you give me a call sometime?"

And she did. About a week later.

"What are you doing this weekend?"

"I'm going to take my nephew to the Paul Bunyan Amusement Center," I said. "Why don't you call back again sometime?" And I really wanted her to.

"Or you could call me," she said, realizing that the thought probably hadn't occurred to me.

She called back about two weeks later. "What are doing this weekend?" she asked again.

"I'm going to put new skirting around my trailer, and it's going to take the entire weekend."

I was telling the truth, but I felt terrible and relieved at the same time.

"Oh..., " she said. "Well, give me a call sometime, if you get a chance."

I never got the chance. School started, and things got hectic. I had found victory in many areas in my life that had caused me such pain. I had gained a healthy amount of weight because I was eating sensibly and no longer starving and abusing my body. Taco Towne had gone out of business, most likely due to losing one of their best customers. I was part of a Christian fellowship group where honesty was encouraged and judgment was left for Christ. I still struggled with playing the part of the hero and found myself too often unable to relax because of a continued desire for perfection. I continue to grow in those areas to this day.

I never took the time to call Gymnasia and wondered if her calls to me had been the calls of a nice young lady who simply was being friendly, or if she really saw someone in me that she found appealing.

I remembered what Julie had said, "You'd be kinda cute if you lost a hundred pounds." Well, Julie, I had lost more than a hundred pounds. Did that mean I was a step above "kinda cute"?

As several weeks of the new school year passed, I began to regret that I hadn't asked Gymnasia out. I debated about calling her, but fear prevented me. Then something happened that made a telephone call unnecessary.

I left school one Friday night to watch the football game between the Warriors and the Crosby-Ironton Rangers. I decided I would stop for a bite to eat at a restaurant before driving to Crosby to see the game. I chose a restaurant where I could get a good salad. I had just begun to eat, when Gymnasia and her mother came into the restaurant. They were given a seat in the booth next to mine.

"Hi, Guy," Gymnasia said, obviously happy to see me.

I was equally happy to see her.

"Hi, Tammy," I said. (Tammy Fordyce was her real name.)

Tammy introduced me to her mother, Ruth, who remembered me from "A Funny Thing Happened on the Way to the Forum."

"What are you doing tonight?" Ruth asked.

"I'm going to the football game in Crosby."

Ruth didn't miss a beat. "Well, Tammy, you love football, don't you?"

"You don't want to go to the football game with me, do you?" It was really more of a statement than a question.

"I love football!" Tammy answered.

I felt like a fool. "You don't want to go to the football game with me, do you?" I asked.

"I'd love to!" Tammy replied.

We went to the football game, and I had a miserable time. I had been in many plays in my life—usually in the role of a clown—but all of a sudden I found myself in a most unusual role—leading man, and I was extremely nervous. I expected bad reviews.

On the way home from the game, Tammy broke the silence in the car: "What's wrong? Don't you like me?"

"Yes! *No!* I mean, yes, I like you—a lot. . ." And then I remembered that I read somewhere in college that the best way to confront fear is to face it head on and admit it.

So I gathered my courage and said, "You frighten me!"

Tammy was shocked, taken back, "I frighten you? For heaven's sake, why?"

"You're so beautiful," I blurted out, "and I'm so. . ." and then my courage expired as I could not bring myself to admit my own insecurity.

After a few moments of silence, I took my eyes from the road ahead to glance over at Tammy. Her face was flushed, and her brown eyes were alive with an inviting softness. Her eyes caught mine, and our eyes communicated in a way that words were unable to.

When the words finally came, they were Tammy's: "You caught my eye the first time I saw you. I wasn't sure what to think of you at first. Pretty soon I realized that I was quite taken with you. You think I'm pretty; well, I think you're someone very special, and you're very good-looking."

She seemed to mean it. I had a hard time accepting it. I decided to confess further: "I don't know much about dating."

Tammy answered: "I'll teach you everything you need to know."

She did, too. It took three years for me to work through my insecurity and my fear and to accept Tammy's love for me.

I had to be sure. Was this the woman God had intended for me? Was this the one with whom I would raise a family? How could you ever be sure?

God showed me again and again that Tammy was to be my wife. Again and again I allowed my fear to prevent me from asking for her hand in marriage. During this time we continued to grow together in our Christian walk. I loved this woman more and more. Her patience. Her understanding. Her sense of humor. Her spirit and her soul. It was as if God said: "Marriage doesn't mean less of these things, it means more."

I prayed for weeks. Finally I decided.

On New Year's Eve, 1980, while we were eating dinner, I nonchalantly looked across the table and asked Tammy, "How much vacation time do you have saved up?"

"A couple of weeks. Why?"

"Oh, I thought it would be fun to do something this summer."

"Yeah, it would," Tammy answered.

"What are you doing in June?" I asked.

"I don't have any definite plans," she said.

"Well, how would you like to get married?" I had rehearsed this in my mind a million times, but now as I reached across the table and grabbed her hand, I realized I hadn't prepared myself for the possibility of rejection.

The tears rolled from the eyes I adored and she answered, "I'd love that very, very much."

"I love you, Tammy, and I want you to be my wife." Now it was my turn to cry.

The waitress approached our table to check to see how we were doing on our dinners, but as she saw us holding hands and crying, she walked right on by.

Tammy and I were married the following June. Tammy's mother, Ruth, married my father in August.

Just for the record, Tammy really didn't like football. But I'm sure glad she accompanied me to the game in Crosby.

After I was chosen Teacher of the Year in 1986, *Star* tabloid sent a reporter to Brainerd to do a feature story about me. I had never seen *Star*, so when I heard they were sending a reporter, I looked at a copy in one of the local grocery stores.

After looking over the issue, which had numerous stories about famous people and their escapades, I was just a little anxious about what it would write about me. I could envision the headline: "Teacher of the Year Married to His Sister!"

Actually, I was pleased with the article in *Star*. Tammy, though, wasn't real fond of the last sentence in the article: "Guy is married to a pretty amateur actress named Tamara."

Tammy wasn't sure if the intent of the story was to classify her as "pretty" or "pretty amateur."

Tammy gave birth to Seth (our nephew) in 1982. Luke (nephew number two) was born in 1984. Jessica (our first niece) joined the family in 1987. And Zachary (nephew number three), whom Tammy insists is our last, came right before Christmas in 1989.

Each summer we take the children to the Paul Bunyan Amusement Center to see Paul. I'm looking forward to Paul meeting Zachary for the first time. We'll probably go on Sunday after a good roast beef dinner. Although Tammy has taught me how to make gravy, I'll let her make it.

As we enter the Paul Bunyan Center to see the world's largest animated talking man, Paul will lift his giant arm and say, "There's the Doud family." And he'll call all of our children by name.

It will be a great day. We will go on lots of rides, and I'll probably get sick on hot dogs. We'll ride the Ferris wheel. When we stop at the top, I'll look north to the building that once housed Taco Towne, where I used to eat spaghetti and chicken and spend the evening with my substitute family.

What Do You Want for Christmas?

Christmas was coming.

I looked for the box marked "Christmas Decorations" and finally found it under five other boxes of things we had intended to sell at a garage sale that never happened. I brought the decorations into the house and suggested to Tammy, who was cooking in the kitchen, "Let's go pick out our tree after supper."

She added a little seasoning to the spaghetti sauce and said, "Remember last year, we put the tree up right after Thanksgiving, and by Christmas almost every needle had fallen off."

She was right.

"Well, it must have been cut in August or something," I said. "We'll be sure to get a fresh tree this year."

"I never thought I would get all the needles out of the carpet."

It had been terrible. Tammy, who had done the vacuuming, knew just how terrible and wanted to remind me.

"You would walk by that tree, and five hundred needles would decide they preferred it on the floor. It was terrible! I've never seen a sicker-looking tree. You put 'Silent Night' on the stereo, and the tree rained needles in accompaniment."

My wife has quite a sense of humor.

"By Christmas morning the tree was naked except for the lights, tinsel and decorations," Tammy reminded me, and although she exaggerated a bit, the tree *had* looked like a man without a shirt but wearing a necktie.

As Tammy and I stood there discussing whether or not it was too early to put up the tree, Seth entered the kitchen.

"Mommy, can we put up the Christmas tree tonight? Daddy says we can," he asked, with his big brown eyes begging for a yes.

Luke ran up to join the three of us.

Tammy stared at her three men. "I suppose so," she yielded.

"Goodeee!" Seth screamed.

Luke smiled, knowing something fun was going to happen.

"We'll make sure we get a fresh tree," I said, as I went to put a Christmas album on the stereo.

I picked out an album with my favorite carols and put it on the turntable. When I hear Christmas carols, something happens inside me. Perhaps you know what I mean.

"That's the same album that made the needles fall off," Tammy announced, right before telling us to come for supper.

After supper, we went looking for a tree. We checked several tree lots until we found a tree that was beautifully shaped. Tammy and the kids agreed this would be the tree that would share our celebration.

I asked the man holding the tree up for our inspection, "This tree wasn't cut in August or anything, was it? Last year our tree lost some of its needles."

Tammy just looked at me.

"They don't come any fresher than this unless you cut it yourself," he answered.

"We'll take it."

We loaded the tree into the trunk and set off for home.

As we decorated the tree that evening, I realized Tammy and I were creating memories for our children. I thought back to when I was a child and helped decorate our family's tree. Mom would remind me repeatedly to put only one strand of tinsel on at a time.

I heard her voice as I said to Seth later, "Only one strand at a time, honey."

"Okay, Dad," he answered, his voice filled with the sincere enthusiasm of Christmas.

As I looked at Seth and Luke, I could see Christmas in their eyes. It was the look of excitement, anticipation, hope.

I unwrapped an ornament as Tammy finished stringing the lights on the tree.

"Seth, come here," I said. The ornament I had just unwrapped bore the inscription, "Baby's First Christmas 1982." "We bought that for you for your first Christmas."

"Does Luke have one, too?" he asked, children being the greatest lobbyists for equality.

"Yeah, he has one here somewhere," I answered.

As I helped Seth hang his ornament on the tree, I felt a touch of melancholy to think of how quickly he and Luke were growing.

"How long is it till Christmas, Mom?" Seth asked.

"It's still almost a whole month away, honey," she answered.

"How many 'Sesame Street' programs is that?" Seth often judged time this way.

"Many, many, many," said Tammy with a laugh.

I joined in the laughter, picking Luke up in one arm and Seth in the other.

"Let's put the stockings on the fireplace," I said.

As we hung the stockings, I asked, "Have you thought about what you would like for Christmas?"

It was a question that used to consume months of my childhood, but now, as I helped my sons put their stockings on the fireplace, I realized that because of the first Christmas in Bethlehem I had everything. God had given us His Son, and He had given us one another.

I prayed that Tammy and I could teach that to our children, and I longed to teach it to my students whose lives seemed to lack purpose and meaning.

Several weeks later, I asked my sophomores to write a paragraph answering the question, "What do you want for Christmas?"

"I want a Lambrogeeknee," wrote John, spelling it just that way.

"I'd like a two-week vacation at the French Riviera," wrote Jennifer.

"I want a four-wheeler," wrote Stu.

"I want to pass this class," wrote Ralph.

"What do you want for Christmas, Mr. Doud?" asked a girl.

I figured this was my chance to explain what I valued. I answered, "I want things money can't buy."

"Like what?" she asked.

"When I was in high school, something happened to me that changed the way I thought of Christmas."

My students could tell a story was coming on, and they are usually more than ready to listen, especially if it means putting class work aside for a time.

"I used to play Santa Claus for the City of Staples. I took the role seriously because Santa seemed like such a part of Christmas in our little community that many people felt it wouldn't be Christmas if he weren't there. The Staples Chamber of Commerce provided me with a Santa suit, and I glued on fake eyebrows and colored my eyelashes. Unlike some Santas, I didn't need to add a pillow to my stomach."

My students laughed. I love the sound of their laughter. I continued, "I was following in my father's footsteps. He had been the Staples Santa for about six years prior to my taking over the responsibility. I had grown bigger than my father, and with all my acting experience in high school, Dad felt I would make a better Santa, so he suggested to the local Chamber that I relieve him of his Santa duties.

"I, of course, was excited for the opportunity, and the extra money would help me buy some Christmas gifts for my family."

Most of the students seemed to enjoy my stories, and I relished telling them.

I sat down on the edge of a desk. "One aspect of being Santa that I particularly enjoyed was arriving in town. The local Chamber of Commerce felt that the arrival should be spectacular, so they arranged for Santa to come by train or plane. They would notify the entire Staples area when and how Santa would arrive. I had enjoyed it when Santa, who looked a lot like my Dad, arrived by plane. I figured Santa was a brave man to come to Staples in that small single-engine crop duster."

"You couldn't tell that Santa was your dad?" one of the boys asked.

"I didn't want him to be my dad. I wanted to believe, don't you see? Of course, Dad would later admit when I confronted him that he had been the town Santa."

"Did you sit on his lap and everything?" a girl asked.

"Yep. I sat on his lap and everything. His breath even smelled like my father's."

The kids laughed.

I continued, "Well, in just a few short years I had graduated from being one of the kids waiting in line to sit on Santa's lap, to being the man in the red suit to whom children brought their Christmas wish lists.

"When I was asked to play Santa, I wondered how they would have me arrive in town. I hoped it would be by plane, because I had never flown before. If I didn't come by plane, I could see myself rolling into town on the train and being greeted at the depot by a throng of cheering children.

"How many of you have never been up in a plane?" I asked, surprised at the large number of hands that were raised.

"Did you get to come by plane, Mr. Doud?" a girl asked.

"Well, I was supposed to, but the plane wouldn't start. No trains were due to arrive in town, so one of the members of the local Chamber of Commerce arranged for the firemen to get out a fire truck. My maiden voyage was in the back of a hook-and-ladder truck with the fireman announcing, 'Here comes Santa Claus! Here comes Santa Claus!' over the fire truck's speaker system."

I paused in my narrative just long enough to invite one of the jokers in the class to sing "Here comes Santa Claus!"

He stopped as soon as I started to talk again. "My father led the way in the police car, occasionally sounding the siren, as we pulled up in front of the Staples Theater. The word was out that Santa would not be arriving by plane as planned, and so all the children met me at the Staples Theater.

"Before I even got out of the truck, they started shouting, 'Where's Rudolph?' 'Where are your reindeer?' 'What happened to your plane?'

"I saw my brother, Patrick, in the crowd, and I don't think he knew it was me. I made my way into the theater, where soon these screaming kids could scream along with the Three Stooges.

"I practiced a few 'Ho! Ho! Ho's!' as I walked to my seat in the lobby. I used a lower voice than normal and tried to sound about the age of my grandfather, whom I figured was about the right age for Santa Claus."

I demonstrated one of my "Ho! Ho! Ho's!" for the class. "What do you think, pretty convincing?" I asked.

"You're not fat enough to be Santa anymore," one of my students answered.

"I looked at the line of kids waiting to sit on my lap. I grabbed the first little girl in line and set her on my right knee. She had her list in her hand. It even included her name and address and telephone number. I guess if I couldn't bring what she wanted I was supposed to call."

I explained some of the different requests Santa had heard. The students listened well, no doubt remembering a time not all that long ago when they, too, were children on Santa's lap.

"A little girl in a white fur coat jumped up on my lap. Many children were hesitant about sitting on my lap. Many could never get out a word, but this little princess started right in: 'I want an Easy Bake oven. A Barbie and Ken doll set. Clothes for them. Dishes. A new bike like my sister's. A mini-snowmobile . . .' She went on and on.

"I told her I would see what I could do.

"She jumped off my lap, and I noticed the next two children in line. They stood holding hands, a sharp contrast to the little girl in the fur coat. The boy's coat was torn and dirty. The girl, obviously his sister, wore a coat that was once pink. I noticed the holes in the boy's tennis shoes and wondered why he wasn't wearing boots.

" 'Do you want to come sit on Santa's lap?' I asked.

"They nodded. I lifted the girl and put her on my left leg, and the boy I put on the right.

" 'What do you want for Christmas?' I asked.

"They exchanged looks. Both had sad brown eyes. 'You tell him,' said the boy to his sister.

" 'No. You tell him,' replied the girl."

I looked at the class.

I continued slowly, "The boy looked at me with his big brown eyes and said, 'We want our daddy to come home for Christmas.'

" 'Oh, where is your daddy?' I asked."

I saw some of my students look down at their desks.

"The little girl looked at me and said, 'Our daddy is in prison.' "

I paused, allowing the moment to sink in, before I admitted to my sophomores that Santa's eyes had filled with tears. I looked around my classroom.

"Did those kids get to see their father?" asked the girl who had asked me what I wanted for Christmas.

"I don't know. I don't think so."

I paused long before continuing: "But that's why I say I want something for Christmas that money can't buy. It's something we've already been given. It's what was given at Christmas to begin with. It's the gift of love, and it's what Christmas is all about."

I left school that day wondering what kind of Christmas my students would have. I prayed that they would know the joy of Christ that is Christmas.

When I got home, Seth came running to greet me with a hug and kiss. Luke wasn't far behind, but his little legs didn't allow him to run as fast.

"Hi, honey," Tammy yelled from the kitchen.

I carried Seth and Luke toward the kitchen. I passed our Christmas tree. It was beginning to lose quite a few needles. I remembered Tammy's prophecy and smiled.

"Dad, how long is it to Christmas?" Seth asked.

I wanted to tell him that it already was Christmas. That Christmas is. It doesn't come and go. It stays around. But I realized he wouldn't understand, so I answered, "It's less than a week away, honey."

"How many 'Sesame Street' programs is that, Dad?"

TWELVE

We Would Have Danced All Night

I finally got to go to the prom.

Back when I was a junior and senior at Staples High School, the major social event of the year was the junior-senior prom. Each year around the beginning of May, the gymnasium was transformed into a tropical island or a lover's paradise. Girls would begin to think about their prom dresses a year in advance, and the guys would order tuxedos as though they were getting married.

The big question among the guys was: "Who you going to ask to the prom?"

The question among the girls: "Has he asked you yet?"

I listened to those questions. I hated the prom, and I didn't want anyone to like it. Good Christian kids shouldn't go to dances, I reasoned, and was happy that at least a church or two I had heard of agreed with me.

The truth, of course, was that I could see myself at the prom, with Linda in my arms. The gym had become an ocean liner, and we danced gracefully across its deck, the sea breeze causing Linda's hair to sway, the moon casting shadows on her brown eyes. The fragrance of the flowers from the nearby island filled the crisp night. I was very light on my feet for a boy my size. Linda was at home in my arms. Together we were a pair. Fred and Ginger would have been proud.

"Who you going to ask to the prom?" Steve asked me, shortly after Christmas vacation of our junior year.

"I haven't thought about it yet," I lied.

I had tossed in my bed at night thinking about it. I had prayed about it. I wanted to go to the prom, but I knew I wouldn't.

"Have you asked anybody to the prom yet?" Steve asked only a few days before registrations were due.

You had to register for prom so that programs could be made of who was going with whom, and the list of couples could be printed in the *Staples World*.

"I've decided I'm not going to the prom this year. It costs too much, and I've got to save up to go to college."

Steve didn't respond. I felt good I hadn't lied to him this time. I had decided not to go to the prom. I was saving the money for college. But if I had thought there was a chance Linda (who looked a lot like Audrey Hepburn in *My Fair Lady*, which I had seen three times at the Staples Theater) would go with me, I would have sold rutabagas on the street corner.

My mother asked, "Are you planning to go to the prom, dear? I bet lots of girls are just dying for you to ask them."

I found all sorts of reasons to justify my fear. Although I hate to admit it now, some of the girls whom I thought would go to the prom with me were not girls I found appealing. I wanted to go with Linda.

"I'm going to save my money for college, Mom," I answered.

"Why don't you go to the prom? I'll help you pay for it. I think you would have a lot of fun. We'll rent a tuxedo. You'll look so handsome." And Mom really believed it.

"Maybe I'll go next year," I answered.

The night of my junior prom, I helped Mom with the dishes before sitting down to write a report for school. I decided to write on the Apollo trip to the moon.

When I got toward the end of my report, I went for a walk outside to see if the moon had appeared. As I came out of the house, one of my classmates drove by in his parents' car. The car, which had never caught my eye before, shone with a wax job unlike any I had ever seen. Dressed in a white tuxedo, he didn't look like the same kid I remembered sending down the hill when we played "king of the mountain" as kids. And the girl in the long evening gown who sat close beside him didn't look like the girl I remembered playing her ukelele at Lincoln Elementary.

I waved at them as they drove past, but I don't think they saw me.

I walked to the end of our sidewalk and looked up at the moon. Suddenly I was in Linda's arms, waltzing across the deck of an ocean liner. The moon lit the deck, casting shadows like sunshine. I could see my reflection in her eyes, and I could have danced all night.

I stood there staring at the moon, slowly coming back to reality. I wasn't at the prom, and I probably never would go.

The following year when I was a senior, the question arose again, "Who you going to ask to the prom?"

I used the excuse again that I had to save money for college. Truthfully, I decided that a senior's first date shouldn't be a prom. I wouldn't know how to act or what to do.

I admitted to myself that I didn't know how to dance. I had tried to do the twist when I danced along with some records, but I had awakened the following morning with a sharp pain in my hips.

When I told one of my friends who went to a church that doesn't allow dancing, I thought she was going to say to me, "You reap what you sow, Guy Doud!" Instead she had just stared at me and said nothing.

My mom said again, "I'll help pay for it. You should go. Girls would die to go with you. We'll rent a tuxedo. You'll have a lot of fun. This will be your last chance to go."

"I guess I'll never go to the prom, then," I said, allowing my mother to share in my self-pity.

And I never did, until I decided to organize a prom of my own.

One of the things I discovered when I started to teach is that the prom is still the major social event of the year in high school. I've seen some students worry more about the prom than picking a career.

Society has changed so much that, in addition to finding the right person to go with, another consideration has arisen: where to spend the night.

One spring night, I was staying at a hotel in Anaheim. As I stood waiting to check in at the desk, a chauffeured limousine arrived, transporting a young couple who looked as if they had just been married. The young man registered next to me. He told the clerk he had made a reservation for a room with a king-size bed.

When asked how he was going to pay for it, he replied, "This is my father's credit card," handing it to the clerk.

How nice, I thought, *his father has given him his credit card for his honeymoon.*

"Congratulations!" I said to the young man.

He looked at me.

"Thanks," he said, but he seemed bewildered.

"I wish you a lifetime of happiness," I said.

He looked at me and must have wondered who I was.

The clerk who was registering me quietly said, "They haven't been married; they've just been to the prom. We get a lot of kids here on prom night."

Anaheim is a long way from Staples, but from both places you can see the same moon.

I love my students. It would be easy for me to stand in judgment, but a wise old pastor, whom I once thought was soft on sin, looked at me one day and said, "Guy, the best way to brighten up the darkness is to turn on the light."

That's where the prom comes in . . .

As adviser to our high school student council, I worked with the leadership to encourage projects that involved student service. I was impressed with my students' enthusiasm for helping with local canned-food drives and other events to aid charity.

Our "Adopt-a-Grandparent" program had been rewarding for the students who had been involved. They had grown as people by discovering the worth of others. I believe that the true leader is the true servant, and I tried to convey that message to my students. But it never got through to them as clearly as it did the night of the prom.

Tom Rosenberger gave me a call. A friend, and one of the local elementary principals, Tom had heard of an idea at a conference he had attended and called to share the idea with me. I fell in love with it and soon shared it with my student council.

"Mr. President?" I asked.

Mike, the president of the student council, acknowledged me. "Yes, Mr. Doud?"

I started gradually. "I've been thinking of an idea, and I want to bounce it off everyone."

"What's the idea?" asked Mike.

"I think we should host a prom," I said.

"We already have a prom!" answered about thirty students all at once, who seemed to wonder if I had lost my mind. They knew that organizing the prom was the responsibility of the junior class cabinet.

"Oh, I don't mean a prom for eleventh and twelfth graders," I said.

"We're not going to include sophomores!" said one senior boy.

"No, I want to have a prom for senior—" but they didn't let me finish.

"Seniors can already go to the prom," Mike answered, wondering what had gone wrong with his adviser.

"No, for senior citizens. People fifty-five years of age and over. Let's hold a prom for them."

"Why would we want to do that?" asked Mike.

"Let's take the money we've earned this year," I said, "and let's give it back to the community in the form of a gift. That gift will be a prom. We'll invite all senior citizens to come. We'll decorate the gym, hire an orchestra, have corsages for the ladies. . ." I was beginning to show some real excitement.

"If we spent money doing that, does that mean we wouldn't take our usual spring trip?" asked one girl, putting down the mirror she held in her hand.

"We would spend as much of the money as necessary to make this a most special evening for the senior citizens. The orchestra we hire will play the big-band sounds of the twenties and thirties and other dance music. I've already contacted an orchestra, and I've talked with our principal, who thinks it's a great idea. I told him that I thought you guys would think it's a great idea, too." I can be pretty persuasive sometimes. . .

After much discussion, the council voted to form a committee to plan the senior citizen prom. In the weeks to follow, I watched my students become excited about the prom. Some of the young men in the council decided to order tuxedos so they would look nice as hosts. The girls planned their long dresses to serve as hostesses.

All of Brainerd got excited when the week before the prom, Paul

Harvey began page two of his national daily broadcast this way: "In Brainerd, Minnesota, the student council is planning a prom...for senior citizens. That's right! A prom...for senior citizens. The Brainerd students are going to provide an orchestra, corsages, valet parking, free hors d'oeuvres... and ... they are also going to do the chaperoning!"

I had been somewhat concerned about the lack of advertising. My students had contacted the senior citizen centers in the area and had sent out invitations, but when I heard it announced on Paul Harvey, my fears of poor publicity died.

The night of the prom finally arrived. The students had decorated our gym more beautifully than I had ever seen it. It was like the gym I had seen in my dreams when I had been in high school. The floral department at the vocational school had donated corsages, some of the local banks provided the hors d'oeuvres, the bus company that contracts with the school district provided free transportation to any senior citizen needing it. My students had tried to cover all the bases. We sat back to wait and see how many seniors would attend. The prom was to begin at six-thirty. At four o'clock, they started to come!

One of the first to arrive was an older lady with a cane. She stopped inside the door and looked around.

"Oh," she said, "so this is the new high school."

I didn't remind her that the high school was more than fifteen years old.

"I've never been in here before," she said.

Mark Dinham, one of the main organizers of the prom, grabbed a corsage and asked her if he could pin it on her. She readily agreed.

"The prom doesn't begin until six-thirty," Mark said.

"I'll wait," she said. "I want to get a good seat."

"I hope you'll do some dancing!" I said.

"I'll dance if you dance with me!" she replied, looking at Mark, who was finishing pinning her corsage.

He turned a bit red. "Sure, I'll dance with you, but I've got to go home and change clothes," he said.

A few moments later, a couple walked up to the table. "Is this where the prom is being held?" they asked.

"That's right," I said.

I could hardly believe what they had to say: "We're from Oregon, and we're on our way to Wisconsin. We heard it on Paul Harvey yesterday, so we looked up Brainerd on the map and decided to go a little out of our way so we could come to your prom. Are we welcome?"

And people kept coming. By 6:30 when the prom began, more than five hundred senior citizens packed the transformed gymnasium.

But we had developed one major problem. Mike was the first to call it to my attention. I had noticed him dancing with one lady after another. He wasn't able to take a break.

"Mr. Doud," he said, "we have a serious male shortage here."

"What are you going to do about it, Mike?" I asked.

"I know where some of the hockey team is tonight, and I think I could call them and tell them to go home and get their suits on and get over here."

"Good plan," I said.

Soon some of Mike's friends started to arrive. I watched as the lady who had been the first to come walked up to one of the sophomores who had just entered the gym.

"You come dance with me," she said, grabbing his hand before he was sure what had happened.

Mike came up to me. "This is fun. Where did they learn to dance like this?"

Mike and many of my students were amazed that some dances actually had set steps and patterns. I joined in as the senior citizens taught us how to waltz and polka. I had never learned to dance, either.

I was dancing with one of the seniors who had dressed up for the occasion. She had on a beautiful long dress with sequins, and the mirrored ball in the middle of the dance floor reflected light off her dress. We danced. She led.

"If I were about sixty years younger, I'd go after you," she said. I laughed.

"What grade are you in?" she asked.

I laughed harder. "I'm a teacher here. I'm in charge of these kids."

"Oh," she said, "you're so young and handsome."

I didn't laugh. "And you are very beautiful," I said.

"Oh, come on now. . ."

The orchestra began to play a song from *My Fair Lady,* and as I followed my partner, I thought of Eliza Doolittle. Henry Higgins saw an elegant woman when everyone else saw a peasant.

"I could have danced all night. . .," my partner sang along with the music.

"That was a good movie," she added, "but I bet it's before your time."

"No, I remember it well." I looked about at my students, every one of them dancing with a senior citizen.

One older man was teaching a sophomore girl how to waltz. I watched her. I was used to seeing her in torn blue jeans. She was beautiful in a long dress.

When the evening finally came to an end, no one wanted to leave.

Mike walked up to me. "That was the most fun I've ever had in high school."

"You mean that was more fun than your junior-senior proms?" I asked.

"No question about it." Mike was definite.

"What made this so much fun?" I asked.

Without thinking for even a moment, Mike answered, "It really feels good to do something for somebody else."

The following Monday, Paul Harvey, who must have spies all about, concluded his broadcast with this story: "Remember last week I told you about how the Brainerd, Minnesota, student council was going to host a prom...for senior citizens? Well, they did...and more than five hundred senior citizens showed up. The high school students danced with the seniors, and the chaperons report no major problems...Oh, there was a little smooching in the corner...but no major problems. Paul Harvey, good day!"

As I look back on my high school days, I remember my mom telling me that girls were dying to go to the prom with me, but I wanted to go with Linda. I wish I had realized then what I realize now. I wouldn't have wanted Linda. I would have gone with an Eliza Doolittle, and we would have danced all night.

THIRTEEN

Stay Forever Young

My job isn't so much to teach as it is to help students learn." I said it before realizing exactly what I had said. "What's the difference?" one of the judges asked.

I thought for a moment: "You can teach to a wall, but when you help someone learn, you have to get involved with the whole person."

I was being interviewed as one of the candidates for Brainerd, Minnesota, Teacher of the Year. The panel of judges sat around the table in the conference room of the First Presbyterian Church. They represented various groups from the Brainerd area and had been given the task of choosing a teacher to represent our district teachers.

I had sat in this same spot at the end of the table the previous year when I had also been a finalist but had not been chosen. I recognized some of the judges who had also judged last year.

One of the judges held my written philosophy of education in his hand. "Why do you call your philosophy 'The Golden Rule'?"

"I'd like to think that I teach children the way I would like to be taught," I answered.

"You like your job, don't you?" one of the judges asked.

"I'm not sure who learns more, my kids. . .or me." As I said that, I started to think of some of the students who had sat in my desks.

I told the judges about Kelly, the girl in my first year of teaching, who had an abortion and then quit school. I told them about Shon, who announced to me as he came into class that he was going to see his mother that weekend for the first time in nine years. I told them about Mike, who at the end of the senior citizen prom said, "It really feels good to do something for someone else." Then I concluded: "Yes, I love my job. I love kids."

"What is your response to those people who say, 'Get back to the basics'?" a judge asked.

"I say amen, but what is basic? Isn't there something even more basic than reading and writing and arithmetic?"

As I answered, I looked at the judges. Some of their children had been my students.

"Your son was in my discussion class," I said to one of the judges. "Did he tell you about what happened with Kent Soderman?"

She nodded her head.

Kent Soderman was one of those students who taught me more than I taught him. He came into class the first day, mostly bald under his baseball cap, and no one wanted to talk about it. I knew why Kent was bald, but many in my class didn't.

I feel that in all my classes a relationship of trust and open lines of communication are essential, especially in a discussion class. Soon we would be studying the reflective thinking process and researching and discussing current events, but for the first few days of class I wanted my students to interview one another.

I had them draw names to see whom they would interview. As they began the interview process, I encouraged them to discover as much as they could about the person whose name they had drawn.

"Well, what makes you tick?" I overheard one boy asking a girl.

"What are you going to be when you grow up?" a girl asked a boy who had the reputation of being a clown. She placed great emphasis on "grow up."

Two boys to my right were discussing their tastes in music. One liked hard rock, the other was into country and western. One had long hair, a black leather vest and a roach clip earring; the other wore blue jeans, cowboy boots and a seed-corn hat.

I told him, "No hats in class."

He took it off.

They then argued over who is better, Motley Crue or Hank Williams, Jr. They were getting to know each other. . .

An obese, shy boy was being interviewed by one of the cheerleaders. They were from different worlds. I wondered if they had ever talked before.

"Are you going to the prom this year?" she asked.

"I haven't thought about it," he managed to answer.

I looked to the right and saw a student I had last year. He had found his father hanging by a rope in their basement. I wondered if the girl interviewing him knew that. I wondered if she would ask about his parents.

Kent was being interviewed by a boy in a football jersey, who seemed to have difficulty thinking of questions. I noticed him steal a look at Kent's almost bald head.

"Ah, you like baseball?" he asked, noticing Kent's Twins' hat.

Once a student finished interviewing a partner, they reversed roles, the interviewer becoming the interviewee.

Toward the end of the hour I called them back to attention. "Tomorrow you can tell us all about your partner," I said. "But before you go today, I would like to read you a poem."

157

I grabbed a copy of "Please Hear What I'm Not Saying" from my desk. I remembered my creative-writing teacher from college, who first introduced me to the poem. His name was Joseph Plut, but he became known as the "mad hugger" because he hugged his students at the end of each class session. At first many of us were suspect of Joe, but soon we came to know that he was genuine.

"The poem is anonymous," I said. "It's free verse and goes like this:

> *Don't be fooled by me.*
> *Don't be fooled by the face I wear.*
> *For I wear a mask.*
> *I wear a thousand masks—*
> *Masks that I'm afraid to take off,*
> *And none of them are me.*
> *Pretending is an art that is second nature with me,*
> *but don't be fooled...*
> *Please don't be fooled*

I looked around at my class to see how everyone was reacting. Most seemed to be listening intently. I continued:

> *I give you the impression that I'm secure.*
> *That all is sunny and unruffled with me*
> *Within as well as without.*
> *That confidence is my name.*
> *Coolness is my game,*
> *And that I'm in charge and that I need no one.*
> *But don't believe me.*
> *My surface may seem smooth,*
> *But my surface is my mask,*
> *My ever varying and ever concealing mask...*

I continued to the last few lines of the poem:

Who am I?
Who am I, you may wonder?
I am someone you know very well.
I am every man and every woman you will ever meet.

I asked my class, "The poem mentions that we wear masks—one mask for our parents, another mask for teachers, a mask for friends. Do you agree with that?"

"I do," said a girl sitting to the right of me. "It's difficult to be honest with feelings sometimes because of the fear of rejection."

I was impressed with her analysis and her maturity. "Don't you think most of us want the same things?" I asked her.

"Yes," she replied, "we all want to be loved."

She then explained that she had learned a lot about sharing feelings by attending Alateen, which is a support group for youth who have a parent or parents who are chemically dependent.

"We do a lot of crying and hugging at Alateen," she said.

"I had a teacher in college who hugged his class every day," I said, "and we loved it."

I paused before continuing: "I don't think my wife would mind it if I hugged all of you every day."

My class became very uncomfortable.

"Don't worry! You don't have to hug me, but if you ever want a hug, I'm available."

I had said this before to some of my classes and had a number of students who took me up on it. I had also received criticism for it and was aware that some people didn't think it appropriate. I had decided to trust my heart on this one.

"Well, that's all the time we have today. See you tomorrow. Come prepared to share your interviews."

As the bell rang, the girl who had talked about Alateen came up to me.

"Can I have a hug, Mr. Doud?" she asked.

"You bet!" I said, giving her a hug and thanking her for what she had shared. As I hugged her, I saw Kent waiting to talk to me.

"How are you, Kent?" I asked.

Many of us had been praying for him. Two years ago, he had been a student of mine when I learned that he had a brain tumor. He was absent occasionally because the treatment left him quite ill at times. After what had been considered a successful operation, the tumor had begun to grow again, and Kent had to have more surgery.

Throughout the process he had kept up with his schoolwork and maintained a marvelous sense of humor. I was impressed with his courage. I was happy that now, as a senior, he was in my discussion class, and I prayed that the chemotherapy and radiation treatments would be successful and not cause him too much distress.

"I can't complain," he said, "and it wouldn't do any good if I did."

His smile was boyish, although in his answer I heard the voice of many adults in his life.

"I'm really glad you're in my class," I told him. "I want you to know that I'm praying for you."

His gentle spirit had invited open sharing, and he smiled in appreciation before answering, "Thanks. Prayers help."

I put my arm around him as we walked into the hall.

"I'm looking forward to your interview tomorrow," I said.

"I don't think we found out too much about each other," he said. "We talked mostly about the Twins."

"Well, we'll see tomorrow," I responded, as I wished him good day and went into the English Resource Center for a cup of coffee.

Kent was right. He and his partner hadn't found out much about one another. The following day, as the class shared their interviews, Kent went first and told us basically what we already knew about his partner: He was a senior. He was a football player. He had a girlfriend. He planned on going to college and wanted to play football there.

When Kent finished telling about his partner, I asked the class: "Does anyone have any other questions?"

I did this after each interview so that the class could get involved in the process. They asked Kent's partner a few questions, and then I asked him to tell us about Kent.

Kent had presented a massive biography compared to what his partner told us about him.

"Yeah. My partner was Kent Soderman. He's a senior. He plays the saxophone. His dad's a welder. He lives out by South Long Lake and his favorite team's the Twins."

Jumping up after beginning to sit down, he added: "Oh, and his sister was homecoming queen last year."

Then he sat down.

I looked around the class.

"Do any of you have any questions for Kent?" I asked.

No one responded, so I continued, "Kent, I have a question for you. I can see that you don't have much hair on your head."

"You're very perceptive, Mr. Doud." He smiled.

I could tell the class was relieved when Kent answered.

"Well, I know why you don't have much hair, Kent, but some of the other kids might not. Would you mind telling us?"

"No, I'd like to talk about it," and he began to relate his medical history.

The tumor had been discovered in junior high school. The first surgery had affected the use of his fingers, so his band instructor had taped his fingers to his saxophone keys. Kent laughed as he told us about it. He explained about the treatment that he was presently undergoing.

"Does it make you very sick?" I asked.

"Sometimes it's not too good," he replied. "It can make your hair fall out—even your eyebrows." And he smiled again. "But it's just one of those things you have to do."

For a moment I looked about the class before I asked another question: "How have your parents handled this? Has it been really hard for them?"

Kent's smile faded. "I think it's been harder on them than it has been on me. I've come home in the middle of the day to find my mother crying. My dad has always taken great pride in being able to take care of his family, but this is something he can't control."

I had never felt what I felt that moment in my classroom. I looked at my students' faces. They were without masks.

"You know, I think it's interesting that Kent has been living with this for some time. We've come to school with him, and yet many of us had no idea what he was going through. I think we all feel better because Kent has shared with us about what's going on his life."

I looked over at Kent. "Thanks, Kent."

Kent smiled.

"Kent, would you mind if some of the others in class ask you some questions?"

"No, that would be fine," he said.

A girl looked at him and asked: "How long did you say that you've had it?"

"Five years," he responded.

I was surprised by the girl who asked, "Do you ever wonder, 'Why me?'"

"No," Kent said. "I've been in the hospital and know little kids who have died. I'm just thankful for what I have. I have a good family, a great dog. I've been elk hunting in Colorado." Then he looked at the girl who had asked the question. "No, I don't question God. I'm thankful to Him."

A long silence followed before Kent's partner asked, "Do you ever worry about dying?"

Kent didn't hesitate in his answer, "No, I don't think about dying. I think about living. I'm looking forward to graduating, just like the rest of you."

Then he picked up his Twins hat and said, "I look forward to this hat fitting like it should."

He could see that several of us were crying, so he joked, "Who knows, maybe I'll even play for the Twins someday."

We all appreciated the humor.

I was glad I wasn't the only one crying.

The girl who had hugged me the day before looked over at Kent and asked, "Would you mind if I gave you a hug?"

Kent wore a broad smile and answered, "No, I'd like that very much."

She rose from her seat and walked across the room to Kent. He stood to receive and return her embrace. No one had to tell the rest of us to join in this affirmation of love and courage. Spontaneously my students and I joined around Kent. I watched as the young man who had interviewed Kent placed his hand on Kent's shoulder. I could detect a tear in his eye, too. The masks were gone.

As the bell rang to signal the end of the hour, we all stood there, most of us crying. No one seemed to care about the bell.

I looked into my students' faces and realized again the truth of what I had learned long ago: In school, the most profound lessons are the ones you learn about yourself.

Kent wasn't able to complete his senior year at school. His cancer spread, and no further surgery was possible. He continued with his studies at home and in the hospital.

I took a bus load of students to visit him at the Minneapolis Children's Hospital several weeks before he was to graduate. He visited with the students, who entered his room in pairs, wearing gloves and masks.

I sat in the corner of the room and watched as the students approached his bed. He had lost even more use of the right side of his body and could no longer easily walk. I could see fear in the eyes of some of the students. Kent could see it, too. He immediately put them at ease.

Two girls came up to Kent, noting the tubes sticking into his arm.

"You're both looking pretty today." He smiled at them.

"You look pretty handsome yourself," said one of the girls.

"You made my day," returned Kent.

Mark and Brian entered the room as the girls left.

"I hear you guys put on a prom for senior citizens," Kent said.

"Yeah. It was great!" Mark replied, not sure what else to say.

I spoke up: "Kent says he's planning to make it for graduation."

"Really?" Mark and Brian asked at the same time, surprised.

"They owe me a diploma!" Kent said.

Then Kent got serious and asked them: "What's happening back at school? I heard about _____ " And he mentioned the names of two students from our high school who had recently committed suicide.

Mark and Brian didn't know how to answer him. Neither did I.

Kent didn't wait for an answer. "I hear about these kids who kill themselves, and here I am struggling to stay alive."

Mark reached over and squeezed Kent's hand. "We'll plan on seeing you at graduation. You better be there!" He held back the tears.

"I'm going to do my best." As Kent said it, we knew he would.

Kent Soderman graduated with the class of 1985. He had hoped to be able to walk up to receive his diploma, but he was too weak and had lost too much control of his body. He had to be taken to the front of the gym in a wheelchair.

Mr. Hunt, the high school principal, called his name, and the young man wheeling Kent started forward. Immediately members of the graduating class began to stand. The teachers stood. The audience stood. As Kent received his diploma, the packed gymnasium applauded long and loud. Kent's response to the ovation was his typical gentle smile.

Kent Soderman died three months after graduating. The courage he displayed in life did not desert him in death. He taught his family and those of us who knew him that death is not to be feared, for it is not the end. The faith and trust he had in God is the same faith that assures us that we will see him again.

Kent will be forever young to those of us who knew him. Not that youth is so special in and of itself, but it embodies the hopes and dreams we all possess—dreams that can only find their fulfillment in Jesus Christ.

Kent wasn't in my room for the last day of discussion class, but I felt his presence nonetheless. On the last day of class, it's always difficult for me to say good-bye to my students.

Once a student of mine, Rick Hjelm, shared a poem with the class. Actually the poem is the lyrics to a song by Minnesota-native Bob Dylan. I loved the song, and ever since Rick introduced me to it, I share it with my students the last day of class.

"I can't let you walk out of here without sharing with you my personal wish for your life. And if you promise not to laugh, I would like to sing it for you."

By this time most of my students have come to accept me for what I am. Not many of their teachers sing to them the last day of class, but this is Mr. Doud, and he is kind of different, you know. . .

May God bless and keep you always,
May your wishes all come true,
May you always do for others
And let others do for you.

I stop and look at my students who surprisingly aren't laughing.
I start to sing again:

May you build a ladder to the stars
And climb on every rung...
May you stay forever young.

I Touch the Future

Mr. Johnson had ordered the Poo Poo Platter, and I was just finishing my second piece of fantail shrimp when the Chinese hostess approached our table and asked, "Is one of you gentlement Mr. Dude?"

"My name is 'Doud,' " I answered.

"Mr. Doud?"

"Yes."

"You have a phone call at the cash register."

"Probably one of our debaters," said Mr. Johnson.

Doug Johnson had been one of my mentors when I started to teach at Brainerd Senior High School. He was head debate coach, speech coach and National Forensics League adviser. Originally he had asked me to be his assistant. Now he had stepped down as head coach, and I had assumed the position. He was my assistant. But in truth, Doug was still the master.

As I went to the phone, I wondered what was up. I had left word at the desk at our motel that Doug and I would be at the Chinese restaurant if anyone needed to reach us. Our debate team, preferring the dining delicacies of fast-food restaurants, had gone to McDonald's and Burger King.

Like any adult saddled with the responsibility of chaperoning kids, I hoped no one was hurt or ill. "Hello, this is Guy."

"Guy, this is Ruth Randall. How are you tonight?"

"Just fine." I was thinking, *I hope.*

Dr. Ruth Randall was the commissioner of education for the state of Minnesota. I had first met her two months earlier when I had been chosen the Minnesota Teacher of the Year for the 1985-86 school year.

She had helped me assemble my portfolio to send in to the Council of Chief State School Officers, the national organization of all the commissioners and state superintendents of public instruction for the United States.

"Are you enjoying your dinner?"

"Yes, it's very good," I answered, without realizing that Dr. Randall, calling from St. Paul, had not tracked me down to this Chinese restaurant in Fargo, North Dakota, to ask me how I liked my food.

"Guy, I tried calling your school, but you had already left with your debate team, so I called your wife, and she told me where you were staying in Fargo."

"Oh," I answered.

"Guy, I received a call today from Darlene Pierce from the Council of Chief State School Officers. You've been chosen as one of the four finalists for National Teacher of the Year. I talked with Governor Perpich today and told him, and he sends his congratulations on behalf of the state of Minnesota. I want to add my congratulations, too."

I was silent. Finally I said: "I don't know what to say. When will they choose the National Teacher of the Year?"

"Mrs. Pierce said she will contact you with all the details. You will have to go to Washington, D. C., to be interviewed along with the other three finalists sometime next month. The winner will be announced in April."

"I don't know what to say."

"We're very proud of you, Guy."

"Do you know who the other three finalists are?"

"I don't have their names, but they are from Colorado, New Mexico and Michigan."

"When you called my wife, did you tell her?"

"I had to. I didn't want to worry her."

"What did she say?"

"What do you think she said?"

"Oh, probably something about how they must have picked the wrong guy," I said, laughing.

"She's very excited, Guy, and I bet she's expecting a call."

"Thank you so much, Dr. Randall. I'm going to call her right away."

I quickly dialed Tammy. She was waiting.

"Seth says you're going to win," she said. I could hear Seth, our three and a half year old, and Luke, who was almost two, in the background.

"The greatest honor was being chosen locally as Brainerd Teacher of the Year," I said. "But now, one of the finalists for National Teacher of the Year. . ." I really was at a loss for words.

When I joined Doug back at our table, he could see I had been crying. "What's wrong?" he asked.

"That was Dr. Randall; she told me that I've been chosen as one of the four finalists for National Teacher of the Year."

Doug let it sink in for a second and then exclaimed, "That's marvelous! Congratulations!"

When I had been chosen Brainerd Teacher of the Year, I had

learned that the entire Teacher of the Year program seeks to recognize *all* teachers, not individual teachers. Whoever is chosen as Teacher of the Year is but a representative of the teaching profession. I was able to accept the collective honor on behalf of all teachers, but it would have been impossible to accept the honor on behalf of myself. The truth of that hit me as I sat across from Doug and realized that he and many others I knew were far more deserving of recognition for their contributions to the education profession than I.

It was snowing wheelbarrow loads when Doug drove me to the airport in Watertown, South Dakota, a month later. The windchill was seventy-five degrees below zero. I prayed that my early morning flight would be able to get off the ground.

We were in Watertown for one of the last debate meets of the year before regional competition, but I had to leave early to fly to New York, where I would meet the other three finalists for National Teacher of the Year, along with the coordinator of the program, Darlene Pierce.

We were to be interviewed by a writer for *Good Housekeeping* magazine, one of the program sponsors. Each year *Good Housekeeping* printed a feature story about the four finalists.

In New York, we would also meet a representative from *Encyclopaedia Brittanica,* the other financial sponsor of the program.

Once we finished in New York, we were to fly to Washington, D. C., where we would be interviewed by a panel of judges.

Growing up in Minnesota, I experienced much cold winter weather. But this January morning driving to the airport in Watertown, I couldn't remember ever feeling colder. The heater in the school Suburban just wasn't producing much.

Although I wasn't about to admit it readily, I was also afraid. It wasn't the poor visibility that frightened me. A part of me hoped I would be chosen National Teacher of the Year, but a part of me hoped

I wouldn't. Being chosen would mean change. Change is often frightening, and fear can be even more chilling than a hard snowstorm.

I was also anxious about flying to New York's LaGuardia Airport. I had never been too far from home and had flown only a couple of other times. I had never been to a city that "never sleeps," and I didn't entertain any thoughts that I would wake up the next morning to find that I was "king of the hill, top of the heap."

I was worried about how to get from LaGuardia to my hotel near Central Park. I had heard all kinds of things about New York taxis, and this small-town boy, who could always ride his bike wherever he needed to go, was experiencing some "vagabond blues."

Doug helped me carry my luggage into the Watertown Airport. I was pleased to hear the announcement that the flight, although delayed a bit because of de-icing the wings, would depart in plenty of time for us to make our connections in Minneapolis. I checked my luggage to LaGuardia and got my boarding pass. Finally our flight was called.

Doug looked at the small twin-engine plane. "They may need you to be the co-pilot," he said.

"Thanks a lot, Doug. I really appreciate your encouragement," I replied, chuckling.

"I'm praying for you," he said, and I knew he meant it.

"Thanks, Doug; God bless."

"God bless, Guy."

There was just a tiny tear in my eye as I was almost blown away by the gust of wind that hit me when I approached the plane. I stopped at the top of the plane's stairs to look back at the airport where Doug was waving. I waved and boarded the plane.

The plane was colder than the Suburban had been. The portable heater in the aisle couldn't keep up with the frigid air pouring in through the plane's open door, but suddenly I didn't feel as cold.

Not only were Doug's prayers with me, but Tammy and my family had prayed. My family at Christ Community Church had also lifted me up in prayer. I knew that whatever happened in New York and Washington would work out for the best. All I needed to do was trust Jesus.

One of the pilots looked back at me. "Are you the last one on?"

"Yes."

"Well, shut the door," he said.

I thought for a moment and then started to get up.

The pilot laughed. "I'm just kidding. The gate agent will shut it in a second. Just try to keep warm."

Soon we were taxiing down the runway, and once we ascended through the clouds, we were greeted by a glorious sunrise.

Because of a long layover in Minneapolis, it was dark by the time I made it to New York. I went out to hail a cab, something I had never done before. I was surprised to see a long line of taxis eager to get a fare.

"The St. Moritz Hotel on Central Park," I said, calling on my knowledge of taxi scenes from hundreds of old movies and television.

The taxi driver didn't say a word until we got to the toll booth for the TriBorough Bridge, which crosses from Queens into Manhattan. Then he mumbled something that I didn't understand.

"What?"

He mumbled again.

"I'm sorry, I can't understand you," I said.

"Money!" he yelled.

"Oh! I'm suppose to pay the toll?"

In the meantime the toll operator began to yell at my driver to hurry up. I quickly got out my wallet. All I had were two one-hundred dollar bills.

When I had gone to the bank in Brainerd to get money for my trip, they asked me if I minded large bills.

"No, large bills would be fine," I said.

I handed the driver a hundred. He swore at me. It seems the toll was only one dollar.

"I don't have anything smaller."

He swore again.

I checked my pockets for change. No luck.

"Could you pay the toll and add it to your fare?" I asked.

He swore again.

And now the toll operator began to swear at the taxi driver. My driver handed the bill to the toll operator. A violent argument proceeded, most of which I couldn't understand. I doubted that I would ever see my hundred dollar bill or any portion of it again.

Finally the toll operator threw up his hands, reached into his cash drawer and counted out ninety-nine one-dollar bills, my change. He counted them out one at a time.

When we reached the St. Moritz, I didn't bother to ask my driver if he would accept a check or a credit card, because I knew that he would appreciate being paid in one-dollar bills.

Later that evening I met Darlene Pierce and the other three finalists: Russell Lofthouse, a kindergarten teacher at Meadow Point Elementary School in Aurora, Colorado; Jacquelyn Caffey, a reading teacher at Davidson Elementary School in Detroit; and José Armendariz, a bilingual language teacher from Chaparral, New Mexico.

Darlene put us at ease, and soon we all reached a common conclusion: We wished all four of us could share the honor of being National Teacher of the Year.

Darlene smiled and said, "The finalists always feel that way, but only one of you will be chosen."

The next day we were interviewed for the *Good Housekeeping* article. Between interviews, we checked out some of the sights of the

Big Apple. I went walking in Central Park, amazed at this oasis of grass and trees in the middle of Manhattan.

Our last day in New York we taxied—something we did all over New York and which I felt I was becoming a pro at—to the *Good Housekeeping* corporate offices, where we were to take a tour and do videotaped interviews for the judges to view. While I waited for my interview, I read the front page newspaper stories about how the *Challenger,* America's three-year-old space shuttle, was set to be launched.

Russ, Jackie, José and I had talked about the shuttle, because we were excited that on this mission, teacher Christa McAuliffe was going to teach lessons from space. It was a proud day for the teaching profession.

Judy Newman, an assistant to Darlene Pierce at that time, ran into the waiting room where I was sitting along with Russ and José. I remembered the day my elementary teacher came into class crying and told us President Kennedy had been shot. Now, with horror on her face, Judy screamed, "The *Challenger* has exploded!"

We ran with Judy into a room with a television, and we watched as again and again the network replayed the tape of the launch and the explosion. At first there was a bit of hope that maybe—somehow—the astronauts had survived. But then reality set in, and the nation mourned.

There was a strange comfort in one another's silent presence. When we finally did speak, one of us suggested that Christa McAuliffe should be the Teacher of the Year.

The news reports focused on Christa, because she was a civilian. Soon the networks were reporting to the world what she had said: "I touch the future; I teach."

All four of us could think of no tribute more fitting than to know that Christa McAuliffe's legacy of teaching, of touching the future, was our legacy as well. Christa made us all proud to be teachers.

Once we were finished with the interviews in New York, we took the Eastern Shuttle to Washington, D. C., where we were interviewed by a select panel of judges representing major education, business and parent groups. These judges would decide who would be the National Teacher of the Year.

Everyone was still stunned by the *Challenger* disaster, and that tragedy cast a pall over the rest of our time together. By the time we were ready to return to our individual states, we had enjoyed the best of times and the worst of times together. Victory binds people together, but not nearly as much as tragedy does. There were tears as Russ, José, Jacki and I said our good-byes.

We had no idea who had been selected by the judges and wouldn't know for several weeks. Whatever happened, each of us knew we would touch the future simply because we taught.

Molder of Dreams

Mr. Hunt, my principal, stood at the door of my classroom. "Could I see you for a minute, Mr. Doud?" he asked.

I joined him in the hall as my students took a break from my explanation of proper outline form.

"You're going to receive a call in my office at 1:15 today," he said. I could tell Mr. Hunt was excited.

"Dr. Randall wants to talk to you, so I suggested she call back during your conference hour. I thought it would be best to use my office."

I knew why Dr. Randall was calling. At 1:15 I would know whether I had been chosen National Teacher of the Year.

Since saying good-bye to the other three finalists several weeks earlier, I had not spent much time wondering. But in the last several days I had begun to realize that if the president was going to present the Crystal Apple in April as usual, whoever had been chosen would have to be notified soon so proper arrangements could be made.

As I walked back into class, one of my students said, "You won, didn't you, Mr. Doud?"

"I don't know, Mark. I honestly don't know."

"Won what?" asked another student.

"National Teacher of the Year," answered Mark. "He's one of the finalists for the best teacher in America. Where have you been?"

The student was now shocked beyond belief. "*You're* the best teacher in America?"

"No," I answered, laughing inside. "I know I'm not the best. There are over two-and-a-half million teachers in America, and I'm not about to say I'm the best. The Teacher of the Year program tries to pick somebody to represent all teachers, and for that I'm greatly honored. Hey, let's get back to outlines."

I finished that class, operating on remote control. I had been patient beyond my ability; now I needed to know. Had I or had I not been selected?

The word quickly spread around school that I was going to find out at 1:15.

I met Mr. Hunt in his office, and we exchanged small talk as we waited for the phone to ring. I felt as though I were a convict on death row, waiting for a phone call from the governor, granting me a last-minute reprieve.

The phone rang.

"Mr. Hunt speaking." He listened. "Yes, I have him right here."

He handed the phone to me.

"It's Dr. Randall."

I wanted to say, "You're kidding," but I didn't.

"Hello, Dr. Randall."

"Can you keep a secret?" she asked, and I wondered what was up. You mean I would find out but couldn't tell anyone? The prospect seemed impossible.

"I'm pretty good at keeping secrets," I said.

"Darlene Pierce said that the White House likes to make the announcement of who has been chosen Teacher of the Year, so it's supposed to be kept hush-hush until the president announces it. If everyone already knows who has been chosen, the awards ceremony at the White House doesn't get the press it would otherwise."

"Oh," I said, trying hard to comprehend.

"None of the finalists are supposed to tell anyone except those closest to them, people who need to know whether they have been selected."

"Oh," I said again.

"Can you keep a secret?" she asked again.

"I'll try my very best," I promised.

Then she almost shouted at me with obvious joy, "You've been selected the National Teacher of the Year!"

Before I had a chance to say anything, she went on to explain that Mrs. Pierce would be flying to St. Paul the following week to meet with Tammy and me. She would explain what we needed to do to get ready to go to Washington, D. C., for the awards ceremony at the White House.

I was still in shock as I listened, wondering how I could keep this a secret.

"You're not to contact any of the other finalists either, because then it will be known who won."

I had told one of the other finalists I would call as soon as I knew, but now it appeared I couldn't.

"We're so proud of you, Guy!" Then Dr. Randall asked to talk to Mr. Hunt about how my being chosen would affect my position at the high school.

I sat and listened as they talked, trying hard to sort through all the changes about to take place in my life. As I look back at that moment, I didn't anticipate five percent of them.

When Mr. Hunt hung up the phone, I could tell he, too, was trying to anticipate what this would mean, but we decided to forget about the future for a moment and just enjoy the good news. I jumped up and down and gave him a hug. Mr. Hunt reacted with a laugh. Principals don't receive hugs from their teachers very often.

I called Tammy at work. Her boss came to the phone, and I told him that I had to speak to Tammy right away.

Tammy was breathless when she got to the phone.

"Can you keep a secret?" I asked.

"You've been chosen Teacher of the Year, haven't you?"

"You can't tell anyone," I said.

"Have you been chosen?" she asked with increased excitement.

"You can't tell anyone," I said.

"You've been chosen!"

"You can't tell anyone. I just got off the phone with Dr. Randall, and next week you and I have to meet Darlene Pierce in St. Paul to plan for our trip to the White House! But you can't tell anyone."

"Why?"

I explained.

"How can we keep it a secret?" she asked.

"Just do your best," I said.

Before leaving Mr. Hunt's office and returning to my room, I did everything I could to act as though nothing had happened. I think I deserve a Tony for Best Actor. By the next day it was all around school that I had learned I had not been chosen. Tammy, too, returned to work, doing a marvelous job of pretending that nothing out of the ordinary had occurred.

The meeting the following week with Darlene Pierce went very well, and we came home with a list of things we needed to do to prepare for our time with President Reagan.

We had to decide whom we wished to invite to go with us to

Washington. Each one would have to receive proper security clearance before he or she could be admitted to the awards ceremony with the president. Then travel for everyone had to be arranged, as well as hotel accommodations. All of this had to be done without anyone from the press finding out I had been selected.

The Brainerd community and Minnesota as a whole began to get pretty suspicious. Why were all these people from Brainerd booking flights to Washington, D. C., the day before the president was to announce the new National Teacher of the Year?

I received a scare when reporters from the *St. Paul Pioneer Press* and the *Star Tribune* called about a week before we were all to leave for Washington. The word was out. One of the newspapers' correspondents had heard in my congressman's office in Washington that I had been chosen and called the story in to his paper.

I would not confirm that their information was accurate. Both papers said they would run a brief story saying I had been selected. I begged them not to.

I phoned Darlene Pierce and asked her what to do.

"Hold them off, if you can," she said, "for at least another day until the White House press makes the announcement."

That same evening, Jim Sloan from the *Brainerd Daily Dispatch,* our local paper, called. "We have it on the Associated Press wire service that you've been chosen National Teacher of the Year."

I wouldn't confirm it.

Again I called Darlene.

"We've waited long enough," she said. "It won't matter now if they run the story."

The next day I was besieged by reporters and photographers. I didn't accomplish much in school that day, but I did learn another reason I had been asked to keep my honor a secret. Now the spotlight was on me, and there was no such thing as a normal day. My phone never stopped ringing, and I was finally forced to take it off the hook.

President Reagan was to present the Crystal Apple in the Rose Garden on the morning of April 14. Tammy's and my family; friends; many from our church family; my superintendent; Mr. Hunt; the chairman of our school board and his wife; Dr. Randall; Governor Perpich and his wife; the president of the Minnesota Board of Education; and representatives from *Encyclopaedia Britannica* were all making preparations to attend the Rose Garden ceremony.

One thing on my list of things to do was causing me great difficulty. Darlene had said that it was customary for the Teacher of the Year to present the president with a gift from his or her state. What do you give the president of the United States?

My superintendent, Robert Gross, offered to take charge of the gift and suggested we present President Reagan with a life-sized, hand-carved loon, the Minnesota state bird. When Tammy and I saw one of the carvings done by a local artist, we both agreed it was a gift befitting the president.

The loon is a spectacular bird that has a haunting, laughing cry. It flies majestically but swims with equal talent, diving under water and surfacing a great distance across the lake. Its colors first appear black, then green. Contrasted with the soft white of its neck, the dark head gives it a mysterious presence. It would be an honor to present the president with this replica from Minnesota.

When the time came for everyone to board the plane to fly to Washington, the loon, now nicely wrapped in a protective box, would not fit under the seat or in the overhead compartment. It was impossible to check the loon with the luggage, and unlike a small child, it couldn't be held on a lap. Finally, a kind flight attendant, knowing the bird was a gift for Reagan, let the loon fly up in front in first class, firmly held down by the seat belt around its box.

I didn't sleep well the evening of April 13. I lay awake, trying to gain perspective on what was happening. After the presentation at the White House I was to hold a press conference at the Department of Education with Secretary William Bennett. I wondered what kinds of questions would be asked. I tried to imagine what I would say to President Reagan. What would he say to me? I wondered if he would like his loon.

A call came early in the morning. The president would not be able to meet with us in the Rose Garden. Something had developed on the international scene that required his total attention. Other arrangements would be made to have the Crystal Apple presented to me, but it appeared that President Reagan would not be able to do it.

My first thought was *What about all these people who came with me to meet him?*

I explained to Patsy Faoro, the president's appointment secretary, that I didn't care if it was only for one minute, but many people would be disappointed if the president couldn't meet with us. She said she would see what she could arrange and phone us back.

After I hung up, I realized that presenting an award to a high school teacher was probably not one of the president's greatest priorities.

In the meantime, I called everyone who had come with us and explained that the president was probably not going to be able to meet with us. Everyone was understanding, and I was deeply relieved.

About an hour later, Patsy Faoro phoned to tell me that President Reagan had canceled all his appointments for the day.

"A major situation has developed," she explained but was not at liberty to disclose what it was. "However," she continued, "the president would still like to present the Crystal Apple to you. It will not be the ceremony as planned for the Rose Garden, but rather it will be a private presentation in the Oval Office."

Because of the time factor, I was informed that I would not be able to present the president with the loon. Ms. Faoro said if we would be willing to come to the White House about three o'clock and wait, the president would see us as soon as his schedule allowed.

I was elated.

Tammy and I rode to the White House in a limousine with Governor and Mrs. Perpich. We were stopped for security at the East Gate of the White House.

The Marine looked at me and looked at his schedule: "You must be Mr. Doud?"

"That's right. And this is my wife, Tammy. And this is Governor Perpich and his wife, Lola."

"May I see some identification, please?"

We all produced identification. Except Governor Perpich. He didn't have his driver's license with him. Nor did he have any other form of proper identification.

The Marine checked all our licenses and handed them back to us as Governor Perpich continued to search his suit in vain for some appropriate form of identification.

I got out of the car and said to the Marine: "Governor Perpich can't find his identification. Can I vouch for him?" The Marine looked at me and then bent over and looked in the car.

"Mr. Doud says you are the governor of Minnesota."

"That's right," the governor responded.

"You can enter," the Marine declared.

We joined the rest of our party in the Roosevelt Room next to the Oval Office. It was about three o'clock.

About 4:30 Secretary Bennett joined us and told us the president would be meeting with us shortly. The secretary alluded to this being one of the most trying days of Reagan's presidency, and he was surprised this award ceremony had not been canceled.

Finally, we were shown into the Oval Office, where the president stood waiting. One by one he shook hands, and then he spoke to me: "I saw you on television this morning."

I had appeared that morning on "Good Morning America"; I couldn't believe the president had watched me on television.

Then the president quoted what I had said that morning: "When you said you don't teach English or speech, but you teach students, that reminded me of some of the teachers I had when I was growing up."

The president then handed me the Crystal Apple and congratulated me.

In his hand he held what appeared to be a note card. He said, "This is a poem I came across back during my Iowa days. It was written by Clark Mollenhoff, who was a reporter for the *Des Moines Register*. Better than anything else I've read, it explains how important teachers are. If you don't mind, I'd like to read it to you."

What was I to say? "Sure, go ahead"?

President Reagan held the poem and looked me right in the eye. He hardly looked at the note card as he recited the poem.

He said, "It's simply called 'Teachers,' " and then began:

"You are the molders of their dreams.
The gods who build or crush their young beliefs of right
*   or wrong.*
You are the spark that sets aflame the poet's hand
or lights the flame in some great singer's song.
You are the gods of young—the very young.
You are the guardian of a million dreams.
Your every smile or frown can heal or pierce a heart.
Yours are one hundred lives—one thousand lives.
Yours is the pride of loving them, the sorrow too.
Your patient work, your touch, make you the god of hope

That fills their souls with dreams, and make those
dreams come true."

I was very moved.

"Thank you so very much," I said.

The president could tell I was moved. He looked at his note card, with the gold embossed presidential seal, on which he had handwritten the poem: "I wrote this out in rather a hurry, but if you don't mind my chicken scratches, you can have this."

Suddenly one of the president's aides appeared, carrying the loon. He handed it to me and told me that I could present it to the president. It was a total surprise.

"Mr. President, on behalf of Brainerd and the state of Minnesota, I would like to present you with this hand-carved loon."

President Reagan held up the loon, obviously pleased with it, and said, "I have some like this on the ranch; I use them for target practice."

"Mr. President," I exclaimed, "don't shoot this one, it's the Minnesota state bird!"

"Oh, I won't," he said.

On the way out of the Oval Office, Tammy whispered in my ear, "While he was reading that poem to you, I got a really good ashtray off his desk."

"What?!"

"I'm just kidding," she said.

I was relieved. I had visions of us walking outside and getting blown away by the Secret Service.

Once outside on the White House lawn, I stared at the poem the president had presented me. *His own handwriting!*

I would find out later that was highly unusual. I also would discover that Clark Mollenhoff had written the poem to honor his mother's retirement as a country schoolteacher in Iowa. Reagan had used the poem for years and was fond of quoting it during his time as governor of California. He had also read the poem to Christa McAullife when she was chosen as NASA'S Teacher in Space. When he wrote out the poem for me, he inadvertently left out one line of the poem, but other than that, he got it right.

A reporter from one of the Washington papers came up to me to ask if the president had given me any indication of why the Rose Garden presentation had been canceled. The president had apologized but said only that something on "the international scene needed handling."

"Did you know that the president is going to make a special address to the nation tonight?" the reporter asked.

"No, I didn't know that. That must have been announced while we were inside."

On our way to the reception following the Oval Office presentation, a news flash came over the radio announcing that United States military planes had bombed Libya in an attempt to destroy the terrorist forces of Muammar al-Qaddafi.

Reagan appeared on television that evening wearing the same suit and tie he had worn when we had met earlier that day. He explained to the American people why he felt the bombing was necessary.

I listened. He had spent the day working out the necessary details of the bombing mission. British Prime Minister Margaret Thatcher had been asked if our planes could refuel at British bases on the way home from Libya. The president had worked during the day preparing the speech he was now presenting.

As I listened to the president, I stared at his note card. Very few people would ever know that Reagan had stopped in the middle of one of the most stressful days of his life to read a poem to a teacher from Minnesota and to joke about shooting decoys back at the ranch.

I looked again at the poem: "You are the molders of their dreams. . ." I decided that phrase was a more fitting title for the poem than "Teachers."

"Molders of Dreams." That's what teachers are, and I now had the responsibility to represent them nationwide.

Tammy and I called home to talk to the kids, who were staying with some friends from our church.

As I heard Seth say, "Hi, Daddy, did you meet the president?" I began to cry.

I couldn't help but think how overwhelmed I had been in the Oval Office. But then, as I held Tammy's hand while she talked to Seth, I realized how meeting the president of the United States was nothing compared to what it would be like someday to meet Jesus face to face.

A verse from Galatians flashed into my mind: "May I never boast except in the cross of our Lord Jesus Christ. . ." (Galatians 6:14a).

Epilogue

The Christmas Eve candlelight communion service was beautiful. As I served the elements to those who came forward, the pianist played carols softly.

"The body of Christ, broken for you." As I said it, the reality of Christ's sacrificial death overwhelmed me, and I felt goose bumps breaking out on my arms.

"Jesus died for you," I said to the next person who came to the table. "This is His body. Eat of it." I saw tears in the communicant's eyes as the significance of Christ's death became real to her, too.

I couldn't help but notice my family sitting near the front of the church. Seth and Luke in their new suits and seven-month-old Jessica looking like a Christmas package, dressed in red and white. Tammy, who had already been to the Lord's Table, held Jessica in her arms.

As we drove home, I thought about how blessed I've been. I've received many honors and awards and much attention since accepting the Crystal Apple from President Reagan, but I realized that no award was greater than knowing Jesus Christ.

Not only had Jesus given me Himself, but He also had blessed me with a beautiful wife and children. Jesus had shown me His love through common people—people who had molded and shaped my dreams, even when they didn't know they were teaching me.

As we pulled into our driveway, Tammy and I both thought we saw Santa and his reindeer flying away from our house. "Look, kids!" Tammy shouted.

Seth and Luke both thought they saw Rudolph's nose as the sleigh climbed into the dark December night, but Jessica didn't seem to have the slightest idea what was going on.

When we got into the house, sure enough, Santa had been there.

We sat together for a moment and talked about the real meaning of Christmas and that God gave the greatest gift of all when He gave us His only Son.

"That's why we have packages," I explained. "We are celebrating God's love for us and our love for each other."

We read the Christmas story from the Gospel of Luke, said a prayer together, and then Tammy told the kids they could each open one gift. This was a moment they had been waiting for. Their excitement was unrestrained.

Jessica, however, seemed uninterested. She sat playing with the wrapping paper, putting it over her head and playing peek-a-boo. As she uncovered her head, I saw the reflection of the flames in the fireplace dance in her beautiful eyes.

The telephone rang.

"I'll get it," I said and then added, "I bet it's Aunt Renee and Uncle Marvin."

As I went to answer the phone, I realized that usually only relatives or close friends call on Christmas. Most people are with their families, but families who can't be together call one another.

Epilogue

While I was growing up in Staples, Aunt Renee and Uncle Marvin would always phone from California on Christmas Eve to share their Christmas greetings. And now, with a house and family of my own, it was a habit they continued.

"Merry Christmas, Doud's," I answered the phone.

"Is this Mr. Doud?" the deep male voice asked.

"Yes, this is Guy Doud." I didn't recognize the voice.

"I bet you don't know who this is."

He was right. I had no idea, so he told me his name, and then asked, "Do you remember me?"

Unfortunately I didn't. He had been one of my students, but neither his voice nor his name was familiar.

"I'm sorry. Could you tell me a little bit more about yourself?" I asked, hoping that some added information would jostle my memory.

"I had you for basic English," he volunteered.

The basic English class was for students who needed remedial help in writing and reading. I taught the course only one year, in 1975, because our school abolished tracking students with different abilities and mainstreamed all of them the next year.

"Basic English. That means you've been out of school for quite a while," I answered, still trying to put a face to the voice.

"Yeah, I sure have. Remember, I dropped out of your class? You tried to talk me into staying in school, but I dropped anyway."

"I'm sorry, but I don't remember," I admitted.

Silence answered me.

"Well, what are you doing these days?" I asked, trying hard to find something to say and beginning to resent his intrusion.

"I'm in Stillwater," he said and then paused. "I'm in the prison here."

I didn't respond but waited instead for him to continue.

"Anyway, the reason I called is because they told us we could call somebody tonight. My parents don't want anything to do with me anymore, and I thought of you. You were always my favorite teacher. You seemed to care. So I just wanted to call to say, 'Merry Christmas, Mr. Doud.' "

We talked for a few more minutes; then he said he had to go.

"Who was that?" Tammy asked.

"One of my students, but I don't remember him at all." Then I told Tammy about the conversation.

"You never know whose life you're touching, do you?" she concluded.

"You never know," I agreed.

I was noticeably moved, and Tammy held my hand. We sat and listened to the joy of our children's laughter.

You never do know whose life you're touching, you molder of dreams!